221
HUMAN
BODY
ENCYCLOPEDIA

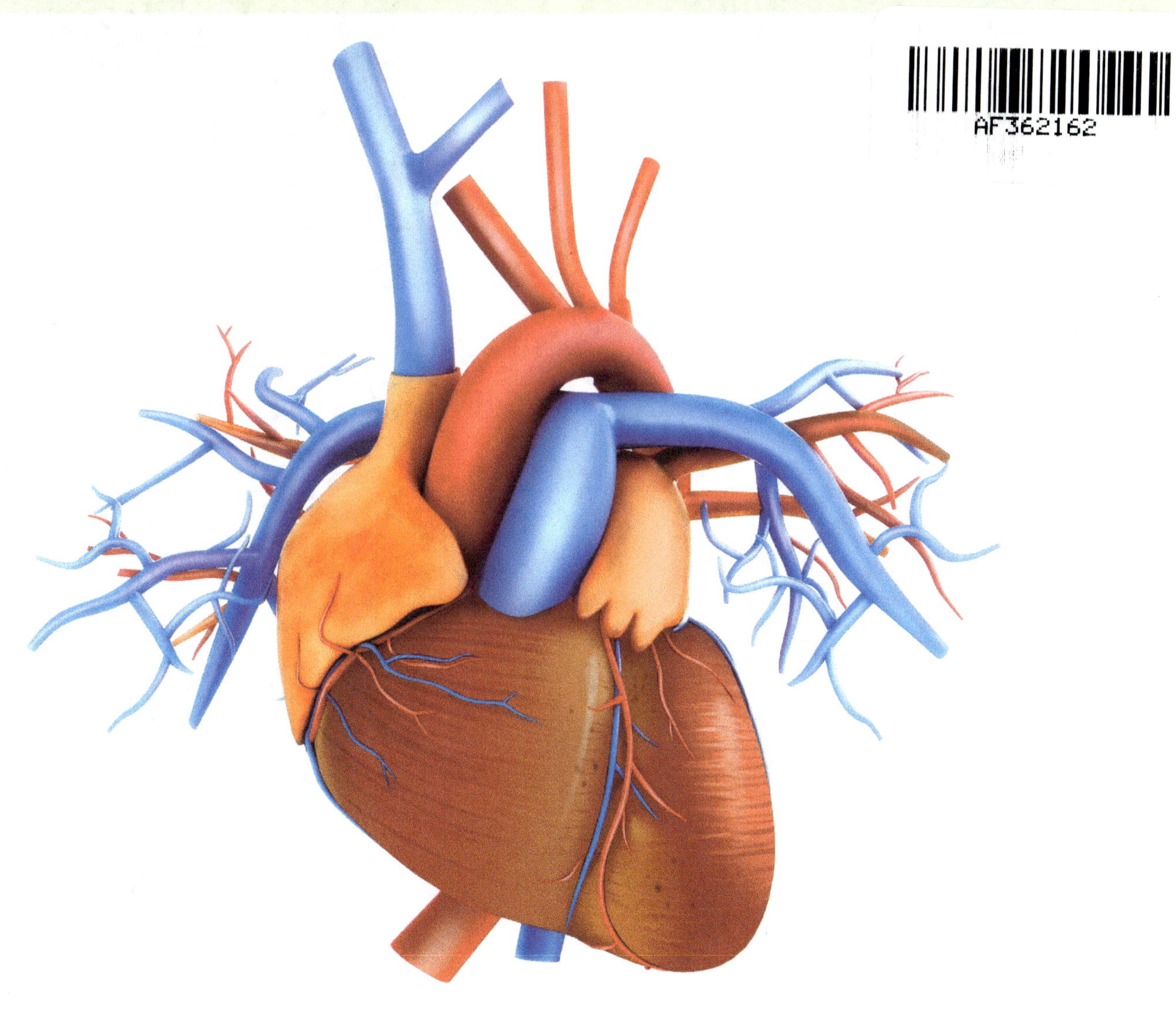

MANOJ PUBLICATIONS

221 Human Body Encyclopedia

Publisher:

MANOJ PUBLICATIONS

761, Main Road, Burari, Delhi-110084

Mob.　：　09999476076, 9868112194,
　　　　　　8178823569, 8178854810

Email　：　info@manojpublications.com

For online shopping visit our website : **www.manojpublications.com**

ISBN : 978-81-310-2359-4

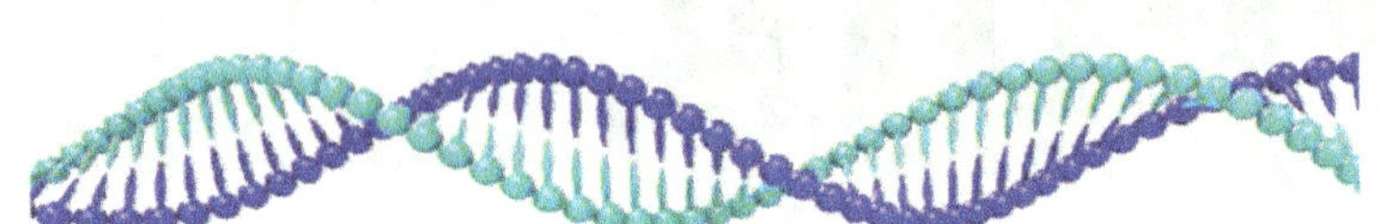

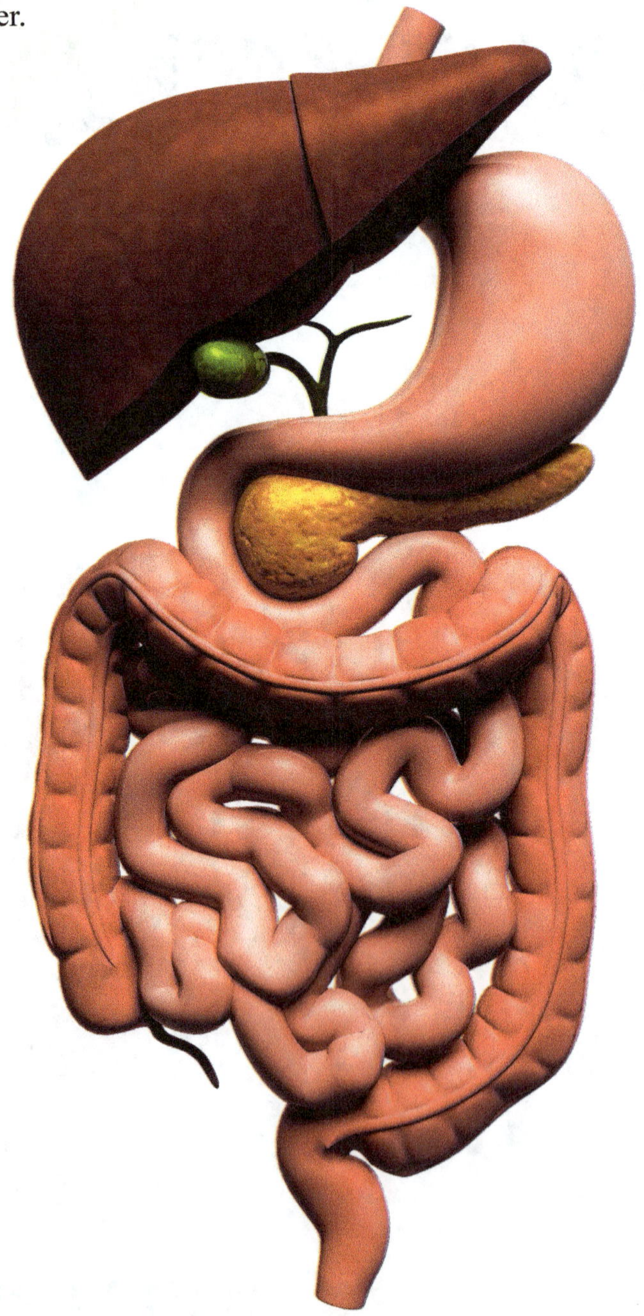

CONTENTS

Introduction — 5

1. Head — 6
2. Face — 6
3. Neck — 6
4. Shoulder — 6
5. Chest — 6
6. Arm and Hand — 6
7. Abdomen — 7
8. Hip — 7
9. Legs — 7
10. Skeletal System — 8
11. Bones — 9
12. Cartilage — 9
13. Axial Skeleton — 9
14. Appendicular Skeleton — 10
15. Skull — 10
16. Ear Ossicles — 10
17. Thoracic Cage — 11
18. Sternum (Breast Bone) — 11
19. Ribs — 11
20. Vertebral Column... — 11
21. Pelvic Girdle/Bony... — 12
22. Upper Arm — 12
23. Fore-arm — 12
24. Hand — 12
25. Thigh — 13
26. Knee Cap — 13
27. Lower Leg — 13
28. Foot — 13
29. Joints — 14
30. Ligament — 14
31. Tendon — 14
32. Fibrous joints — 14
33. Cartilaginous Joints — 15
34. Synovial Joints — 15
35. Ball and Socket Joint — 15

36. Gliding Joint — 15
37. Hinge Joint — 16
38. Pivot Joint — 16
39. Saddle Joint — 16
40. Muscular System — 17
41. Muscle Fibre — 18
42. Cardiac Muscle — 18
43. Skeletal Muscle — 18
44. Smooth Muscle — 19
45. Epicranius Muscles — 19
46. Orbicularis Occuli — 19
47. Orbicularis Oris — 19
48. Trapezius Muscle — 20
49. Deltoid Muscle — 20
50. Pectorals — 20
51. Biceps — 21
52. Triceps — 21
53. Rectus Abdominus — 22
54. Wrist and Finger... — 22
55. Wrist and Finger... — 22
56. Muscles of Leg — 23
57. Muscles of Foot... — 23
58. Circulatory System — 24
59. Blood — 25
60. Red Blood Cells — 25
61. White Blood Cells — 25
62. Thrombocytes — 25
63. Plasma — 26
64. Heart — 26
65. Blood Vessel — 27
66. Artery — 27
67. Vein — 27
68. Capillaries — 28
69. Carotid Arteries — 28
70. Jugular Vein — 28
71. Superior Vena Cava — 29

72. Inferior Vena Cava — 29
73. Aorta — 29
74. Pulmonary Artery — 29
75. Pulmonary Vein — 29
76. Left Ventricle — 30
77. Right Ventricle — 30
78. Left Atrium — 30
79. Right Atrium — 30
80. Tricuspid and... — 31
81. Pulmonary and... — 31
82. SA and AV Node — 31
83. Hepatic Artery — 32
84. Portal Vein — 32
85. Iliac Vein — 32
86. Iliac Artery — 32
87. Femoral Vein — 32
88. Femoral Artery — 32
89. Lymphatic System — 35
90. Tonsils — 36
91. Lymph Vessels — 36
92. Lymph Node — 36
93. Lymphatic (Lymph)... — 37
94. Bone Marrow — 37
95. Spleen — 37
96. Peyer's Patch — 37
97. Digestive System — 38
98. Mouth — 39
99. Salivary Glands — 39
100. Teeth — 39
101. Palate — 39
102. Uvula — 39
103. Pharynx Chamber — 40
104. Oesophagus — 40
105. Stomach — 40
106. Pyloric Sphincter — 40
107. Small Intestine — 41

Entry	Page
108. Duodenum	41
109. Jejunum	41
110. Ileum	41
111. Villus	42
112. Large Intestine	42
113. Rectum	42
114. Appendix	42
115. Peritoneum	43
116. Liver	43
117. Gall Bladder	43
118. Pancreas	43
119. Liver Vessels	44
120. Bile	44
121. Digestive Enzymes	44
122. Respiratory System	45
123. Nostril	45
124. Nasal Cavity	45
125. Sinuses	45
126. Pharynx	46
127. Larynx	46
128. Epiglottis	46
129. Vocal Cords	46
130. Trachea	46
131. Bronchi	47
132. Alveoli	47
133. Lungs	47
134. Pleura	48
135. Diaphragm	48
136. Endocrine System	50
137. Hormone	51
138. Pineal Gland	51
139. Pituitary Gland	51
140. Thyroid Gland	52
141. Parathyroid Gland	52
142. Thymus Gland	52
143. Adrenal Glands	53
144. Islets of Langerhans	53
145. Excretory System	54
146. Kidney	54
147. Ureter	55
148. Urinary Bladder	55
149. Urethra	55
150. Nephron	55
151. Renal Blood Vessels	56
152. Glomerulus	56
153. Bowman's Capsule	56
154. Nephron Tubules	56
155. Reproductive System	58
156. Female Reproductive...	58
157. Vagina and Uterus	59
158. Ovaries	59
159. Fallopian Tube	59
160. Male Reproductive...	59
161. Nervous System	60
162. Neuron	61
163. Synapse	61
164. Motor Neuron	61
165. Sensory Neuron	62
166. Brain	62
167. Fore-brain	62
168. Cerebral Cortex	63
169. Thalamus	63
170. Hypothalamus	63
171. Lobes of Cerebrum	63
172. Brain-stem	64
173. Mid-brain	64
174. Hind-brain	64
175. Pons	64
176. Medulla Oblongata	64
177. Cerebellum	64
178. Central Nervous...	65
179. Spinal Cord	65
180. Peripheral Nervous...	65
181. Somatic Nervous...	66
182. Spinal Nerves	66
183. Cranial Nerves	66
184. Autonomic Nervous...	67
185. Parasympathetic...	68
186. Sympathetic...	68
187. Sense Organs	69
188. Eye	69
189. Sclera and Cornea	69
190. Choroid and Iris	70
191. Pupil	70
192. Retina	70
193. Lens	70
194. Optic Nerves	70
195. Nose	72
196. Nasal Cavity	72
197. Olfactory Portion	72
198. Ear	73
199. External Ear	73
200. Ear-drum	74
201. Middle Ear	74
202. Eustachian Tube	74
203. Cochlea	74
204. Inner Ear	74
205. Auditory Nerves	75
206. Mouth	75
207. Soft and Hard Palate	75
208. Teeth	76
209. Tongue	77
210. Papillae	77
211. Taste Buds	77
212. Taste Pores and...	77
213. Skin	78
214. Epidermis	78
215. Dermis	78
216. Hypodermis Layer	78
217. Glands	79
218. Pores	79
219. Touch Sensors	79
220. Hair	80
221. Nail	80

Introduction

The human body is like a well-organised machine. It is capable of performing different tasks. The human body has a specialised structure, both inside and outside. The body-parts work together to perform several functions in orderly manner.

Cell

The cell is the fundamental structural and functional unit of all living organisms. It is the smallest unit of life. There are trillions of cells in the human body. Different cells have specialized jobs to do. For example, our brain cells perform entirely more different functions than our heart cells. They do one particular job.

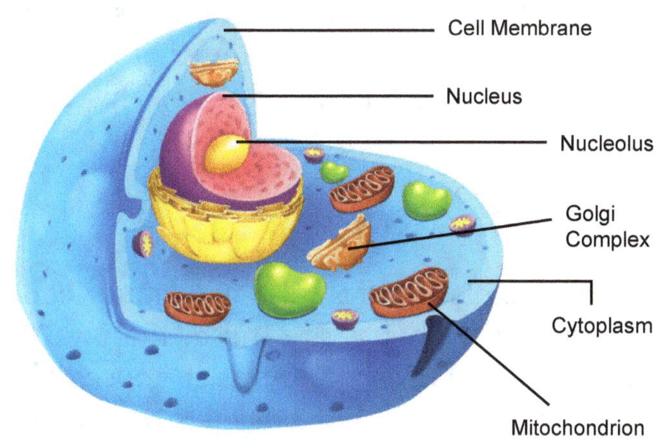

Tissue

A tissue is a group of similarly structured cells woven together that perform a specific type of function in an organ. All cells of tissues have common origin. For example, nervous tissue has nerve cells or neurons, which are the same structurally and functionally.

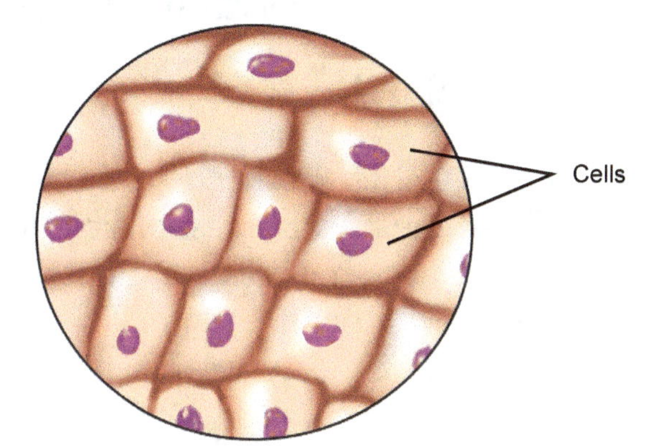

Organ

The different types of tissues join together to perform a specific function. This association of tissues is known as an organ. For example, a human heart is made up of muscle tissues, nerve tissues, blood tissues and connective tissues.

Organ System

An organ system is a group of various organs that work together to perform a specific function. For example, a muscular system helps in the movement of the body.

Organ system	Function
Skeletal system	Support and protection
Muscular system	Movement and locomotion
Respiratory system	Breathing/exchange of gases
Circulatory system	Transport of blood
Excretory system	Waste removal
Digestive system	Digestion and food absorption
Endocrine system	Regulation
Reproductive system	Reproduction
Nervous system	Control and coordination

1. Head

The head includes the part of the body above the neck, principally the skull and the face along with the internal structures. The skull is the bony base of the head that protects the brain. When compared to the ancestors, the apes, human heads house big-sized brains. The size of a newborn baby's head is about one-quarter of its entire body size, but at the time of adulthood, it remains only one-eighth of the entire body size. This is the reason why the newborns face difficulty in holding their heads.

2. Face

The face is the frontal part of the head. It is comprised of the forehead, the ears, the eyes with eyebrows, the cheeks, the nose, the jaw, the mouth, the lips and the chin. It is the highly sensitive region of the human body as it houses all the five sense organs. Our nose and ears keep growing throughout the life, but our eyes always remain the same in size. The facial muscles are one of the most delicate muscles, especially those present in the eyes and the lips.

3. Neck

The neck attaches the head to the rest of the body. Our neck is composed of different types of muscles. These muscles are responsible for the movement of the head. Apart from the movement of the head, these neck muscles contribute to the maintenance of blood flow to the brain, and they also assist in holding the head upright. The spinal cord begins from the neck. The part of the spinal cord in the neck is called the cervical spine.

4. Shoulder

The shoulder lies between the neck and the upper arm of the human body. It displays maximum mobility. The joints of the shoulders help the arms to rotate in a full circle as well as to elevate upward, downward, forward, backward and more. Shoulder movements help a gymnast to perform amazing stunts. But the excessive movement of shoulders while performing manual labour or exercise or sports, can break down the soft tissues in the shoulder region.

5. Chest

The part of the human body located between the neck and the abdomen is the chest. The chest is also called the thorax. The rib cage, spine and shoulder are also the part of the chest. The rib cage protects different organs underneath, including the heart, lungs and liver. The chest muscles support the movement of the shoulders. The chest muscles also play a part in breathing and pulling the rib cage to create room for the lungs to expand.

6. Arm and Hand

Human arm and hand are also referred as the upper limb. The shoulder, elbow, palm and the fingers are the part of the upper limb. The hand bones (carpals and metacarpals) and the muscles help us to hold things. The muscles in our fingers are so strong that only a few fingertips can bear the entire weight of the body while climbing vertical surfaces.

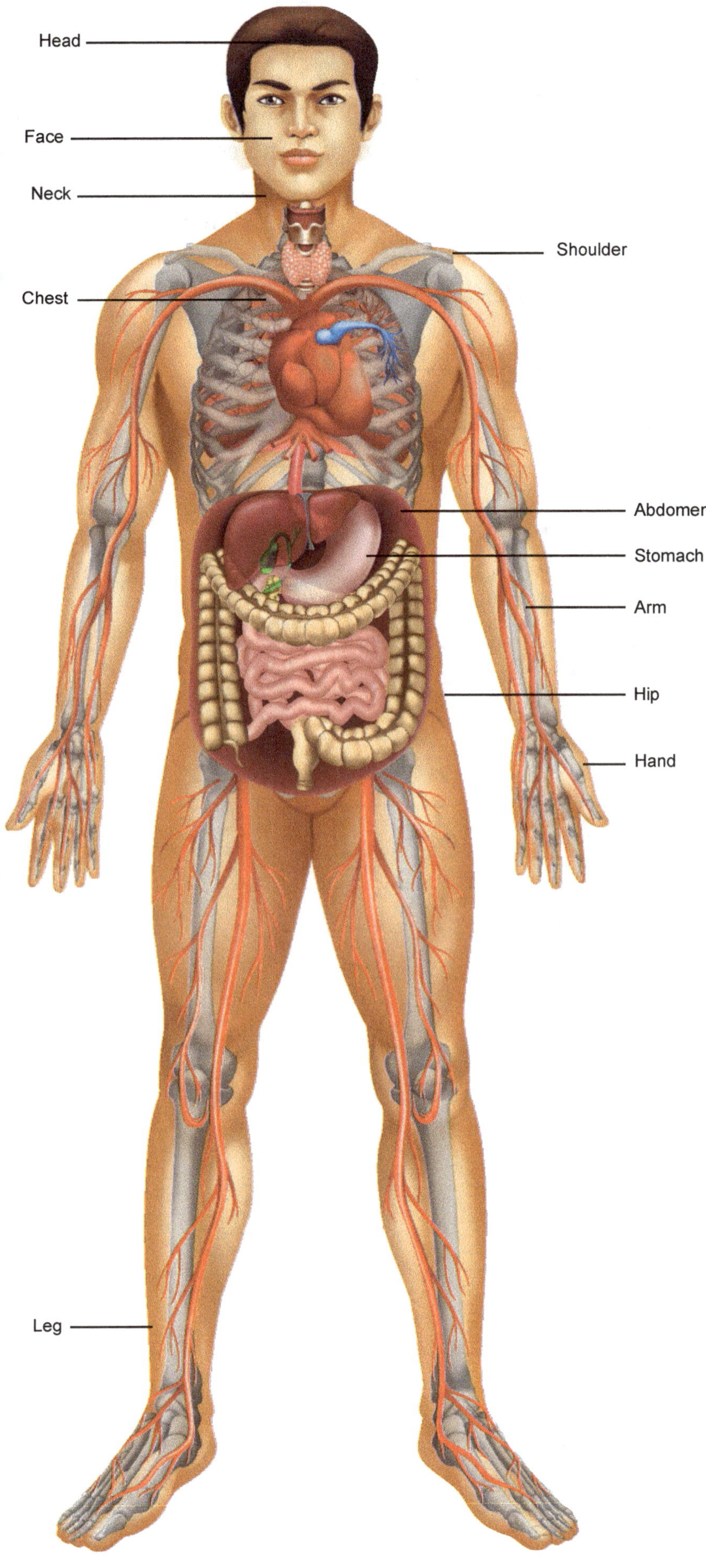

7. Abdomen

The part of the body that lies between the chest and the hip region is called the abdomen.

The digestive system is located in the abdomen. The stomach that is housed in the abdominal cavity can expand to hold up to 1.5 litres of food when full. Most of the movements in the body are supported by the back and the abdominal muscles, such as to sit, stand, bend over and pick things up.

8. Hip

The hip is the lowest part of the abdomen. It is in the pelvic region. The hip bone provides support to the body while sitting. The hip joint is the largest joint, crucial to support various postures of the body. The muscles in the hip facilitate the movement of the hip joint and also provide a natural cushion for the body. Among all the bones, the bones in the pelvic region are different in the males and the females. Females have more fragile pelvic bones than males.

9. Legs

Hip, thigh, knee, lower leg, ankle and foot together form a leg. The leg is a complex structure composed of several joints and muscles. The lower leg has two major bones and 20 different muscles that help in the movement of the leg and the toes. It is researched that the right leg is controlled by the left lobe of the brain and the left leg is controlled by the right lobe of the brain.

10. Skeletal System

The skeletal system is the bony framework of the body. It provides support and protects the soft organs like brain, lungs and heart. It has an important role in the body movement. This system is made up of 206 bones of different shapes and sizes. Bones are made up of living cells. The inside of some bones is soft and spongy. This is called the bone marrow. The skeleton consists of bones, teeth, cartilage and joints. The skeletal system along with the muscles in the body defines the shape and size of the body.

The human skeleton is divided into two parts : the axial skeleton and the appendicular skeleton.

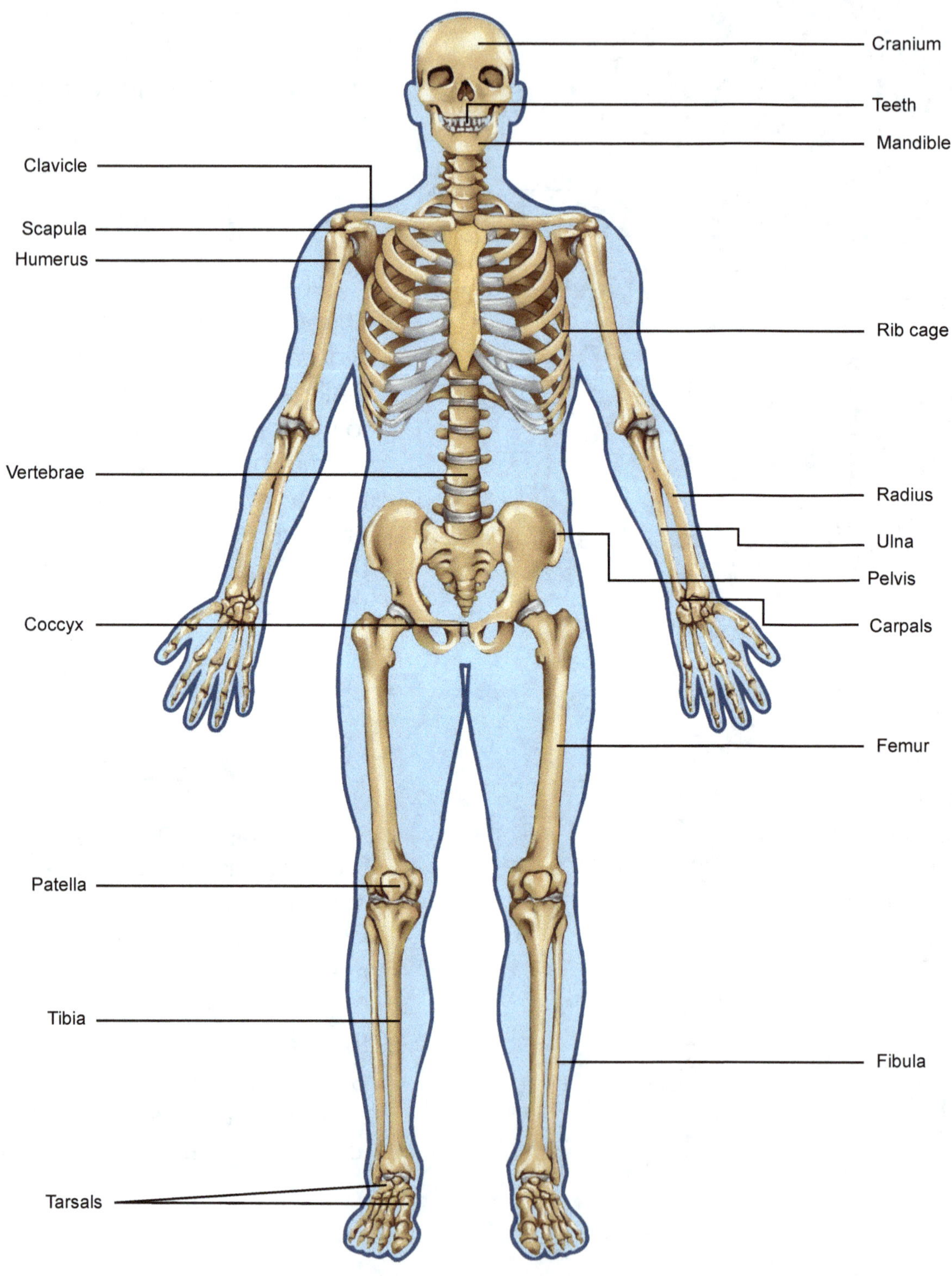

11. Bones

Human bones grow continually from birth till the mid-20's. A growing baby has 350 bones. As it grows, many bones join together and thus the number of bones decreases till the baby grows into an adult. The bones of the skeleton are classified according to their shapes and formations. Over half of our bones are in our hands and feet. Bones keep growing as we grow. That is why we get taller and broader. The biggest bones are found in the legs and the smallest bones are inside the ears.

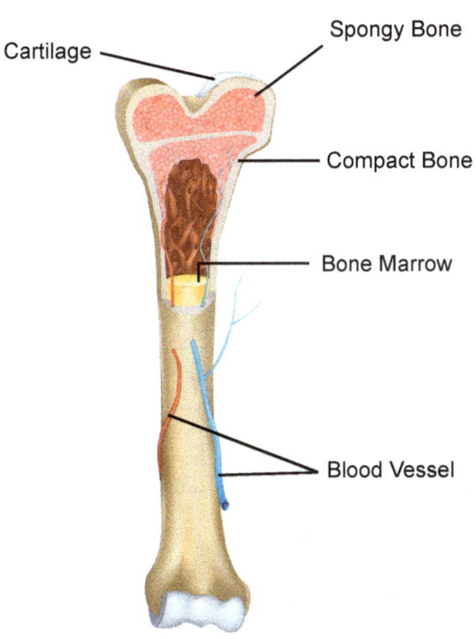

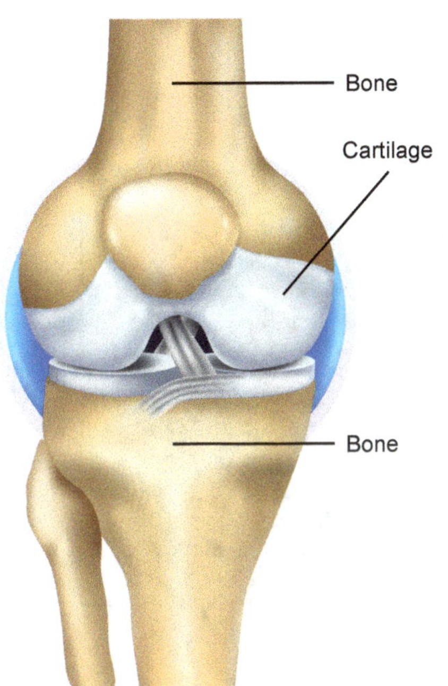

12. Cartilage

Cartilage is an important component of the human body. It is a connective tissue that helps in the structural formation of the body and provides support to the other tissues of the body. It is found in many areas of the body. For example, joints between bones, ends of the ribs, between the vertebrae in the spine and in the ears and the nose. Cartilage is softer and much more flexible in nature than bones, but is a firm tissue.

Without a skeleton a human body would resemble a chunk of jelly.

13. Axial Skeleton

The axial skeleton is the part of the skeleton which is comprised of 80 bones of the head and trunk of the body. Axial skeleton is comprised of the bones of the skull, the ossicles of the middle ear, the hyoid bone, the rib cage, sternum and the vertebral column. It lies in the mid-line of body.

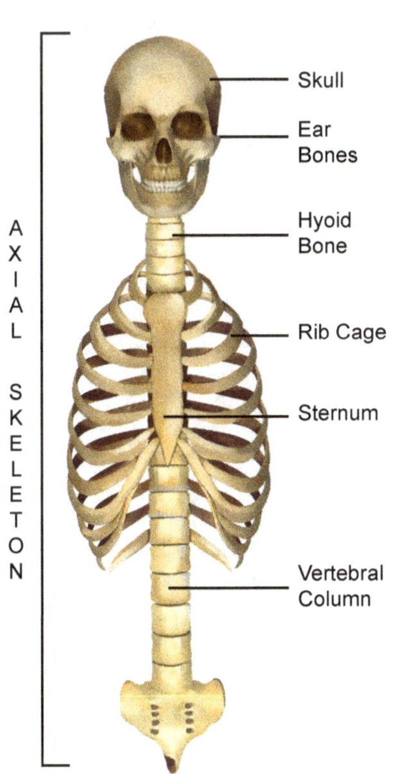

14. Appendicular Skeleton

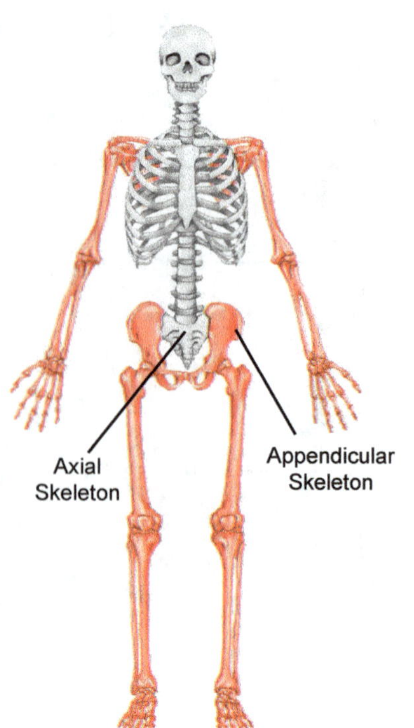

Axial Skeleton

Appendicular Skeleton

The word 'appendicular' refers to anything related to a limb or limbs. The appendicular skeleton is the second part of our skeletal system, which contains a total of 126 bones. This part consists of the bones of the limbs (hands and legs) along with their girdles: pectoral and pelvic. Pelvic girdle is the place where the lower part (legs) of the body connects with the upper part of the body (skull, spine and hands).

Appendages

Parts of body attached to the chest and abdomen, such as arms and legs.

15. Skull

The skull is the bony framework of the head, which gives shape to the head and the face. Eight flat bones join together to form a skull. The skull is arranged in two parts: the cranium and the facial skeleton. The cranium also called brain box, consists of four bones while the facial skeleton consists of eight facial bones on the front. The cranium is the largest part of the skull enclosing the brain, eyes, ears and the nose, while the facial skeleton is comprised of the region around eyes, nose and mouth.

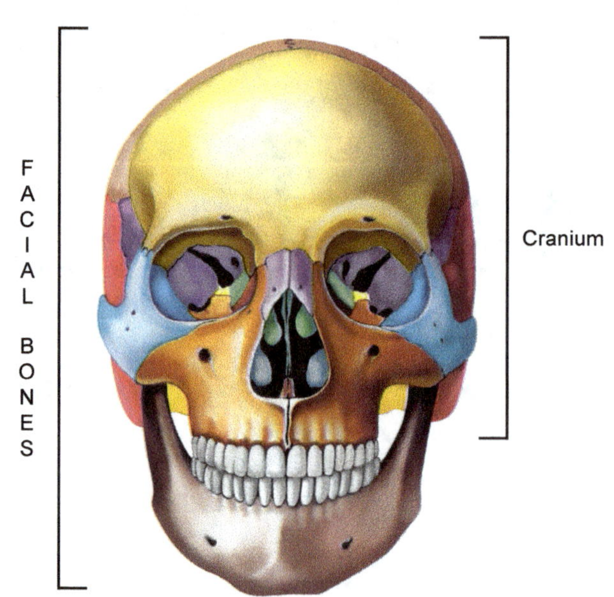

16. Ear Ossicles

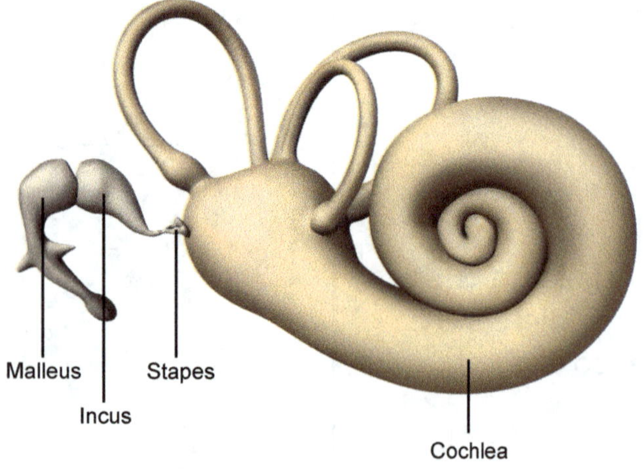

Ear ossicles are the three smallest bones of the body. They are located in the middle ear cavity. They are joined together with tiny joints. The main function of these bones is to transmit sound vibrations. These three bones are named as: the malleus (the first ossicles), incus (second ossicles) and stapes (the third ossicles). Malleus is commonly called a hammer, incus is called an anvil and stapes is called a stirrup.

Ossicles mean small bones.

17. Thoracic Cage

The thoracic cage is also called the rib cage or the thoracic basket. It is comprised of a sternum and a set of curved bones, called the ribs. It is attached to the diaphragm at the lower end. The main functions of the thoracic cage are to protect and support the internal organs and provide a definite shape to the thorax region. It protects the sensitive organs such as the heart and lungs in the chest area.

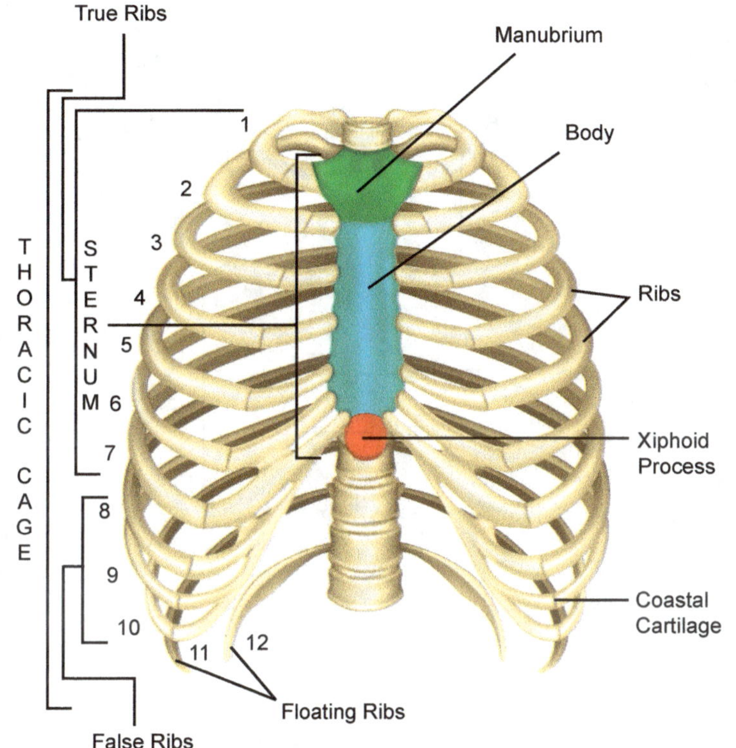

18. Sternum (Breast Bone)

The sternum is also called the breast bone. It is a long, narrow flat bone, located at the middle of the chest. It is divided into three parts: the manubrium, the body of the sternum (sometimes called the gladiolus) and the xiphoid process. It supports the muscles which help in the movement of arms, head and neck, and protects several vital organs, such as the heart, aorta, vena cava and thymus gland that are located behind the sternum.

Xiphoid Process

It is the lowermost part of the sternum made up of cartilage.

19. Ribs

Ribs are the long curved bones, attached behind to the middle segment of the vertebral column/spine. There are twelve pairs of ribs: the true ribs (ribs 1-7), the false ribs (ribs 8-10) and the floating ribs (11-12). The ribs swing up and down when we breathe to inflate and deflate our lungs. The ribs protect the internal organs that they enclose and lend support to the muscles of the trunk.

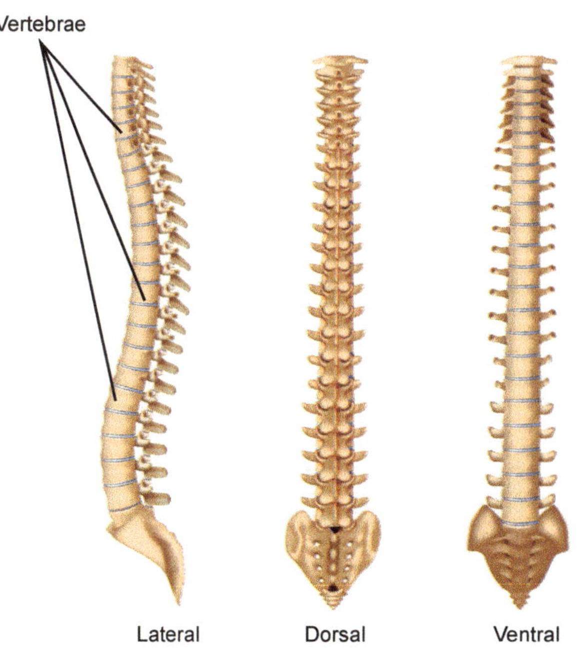

20. Vertebral Column (Backbone)

The vertebral column is also known as the spinal column. It is a flexible structure formed by a number of irregularly shaped bones called vertebrae. It consists of 26 vertebrae in adults and 33 in children. The backbone extends from the neck to the tail bone. The foremost job of this column is to provide protection to the spinal cord (part of the nervous system). Other than this, the column gives an upright shape to the human body, helps while walking and standing and acts as an attachment for many muscles.

A human backbone resembles a spiral staircase.

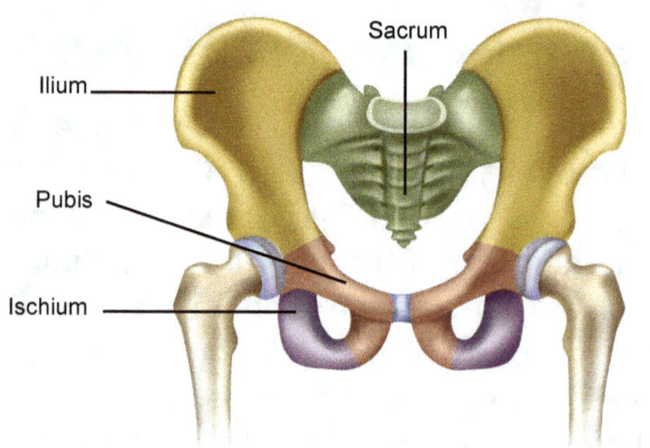

21. Pelvic Girdle/Bony Pelvis

The pelvic girdle is a link between the trunk (upper part of the body) and the lower part of the body. The hip or pelvic girdle is made up of two coxal (two hip bones : left and right) bones. Each coxal bone is shaped up by the combination of three bones: ilium, ischium and pubis. These bones bear the entire weight of the body while sitting. It supports the intestines, urinary bladder and other internal organs.

22. Upper Arm

The upper arm is the section of an arm from the elbow to the shoulder. The longest bone present in the upper arm is the humerus. The upper arm helps pull and lift things. The joint at the elbow allows the arm to swing 180 degrees at full extension. The round socket of the shoulder blade in which the head of the upper arm fits is called the glenoid cavity.

23. Fore-arm

The fore-arm is the area between the wrist and the elbow. The bones of the fore-arm are called radio–ulna. Ulna is a longer bone than radius. The flexibility of the fore-arm depends on the three major muscles associated with the bones, the brachialis, biceps brachii and brachioradialis. The wrist is an important part of this region. It consists of 13 bones along with multiple muscles. The muscles in the fore-arm help in the rotation of the wrist.

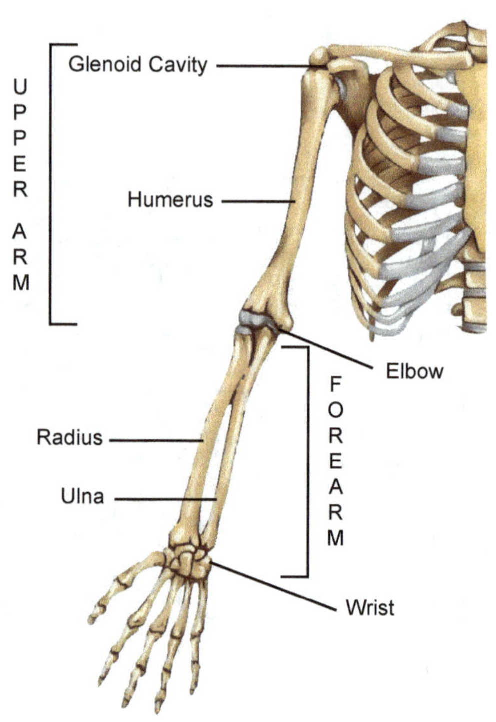

Human hand from the clavicle and shoulder to the fingers is collectively referred as upper limb or extremity. The upper limb motions are very important for the daily activities, such as brushing teeth, drinking, eating, combing hair, washing face, etc.

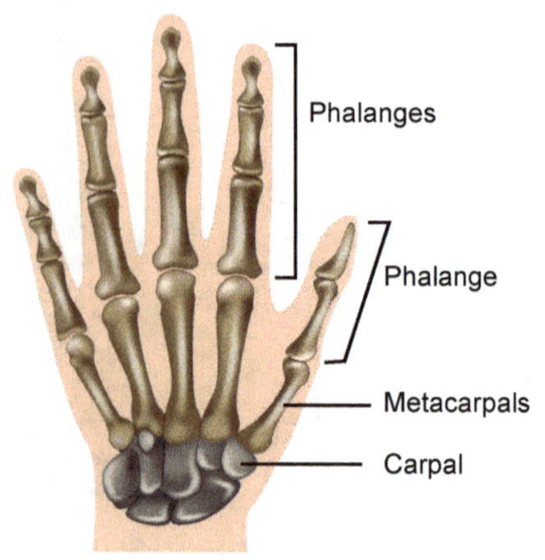

24. Hand

The bones of the hand are arranged in groups. The three types of the bones that constitute a hand are: the carpals, the metacarpals and the phalanges. The carpals or the bones which enter into the formation of the wrist are short bones. The metacarpals (long bones) form the skeleton of the palm of the hand and the phalanges (long bones) are the bones of the fingers. Each of the digits of the hands contains three phalanges (singular: phalanx) except for the thumbs that contain only two.

25. Thigh

The bones of the lower limbs are connected with the trunk by means of the pelvic girdle. The lower limb supports the body; they help to maintain balance and mobility. The part between the hip and the knee is referred as the thigh. The bone of the thigh is the femur bone, which is the largest and strongest bone in the human body. The strong thigh muscles attach to the femur and pull the femur during the movements of the hip and knee joints.

> **The human leg from the hip to the foot is collectively referred as lower limb or extremity.**

26. Knee Cap

The knee cap is also called the patella. It is a flat triangular bone. It lies on the front part of the knee. The knee cap slides up and down as we flex and extend the leg. The front surface of the patella is rough. The cartilage present on the back side of the knee cap provides cushioning between the knee cap and the femur.

> **The knee joint is one of the main joints affected during the old age, when a person is prone to suffer from arthritis and osteoporosis.**

27. Lower Leg

The part between the knee and the ankle is the lower leg. The two major bones forming the lower leg are the tibia and the fibula. These two bones connect the ankle bone to the knee. Tibia forms the main skeleton of the lower leg and fibula supports the muscles that balance the lower leg and the ankle. The tibia bears most of the body's weight.

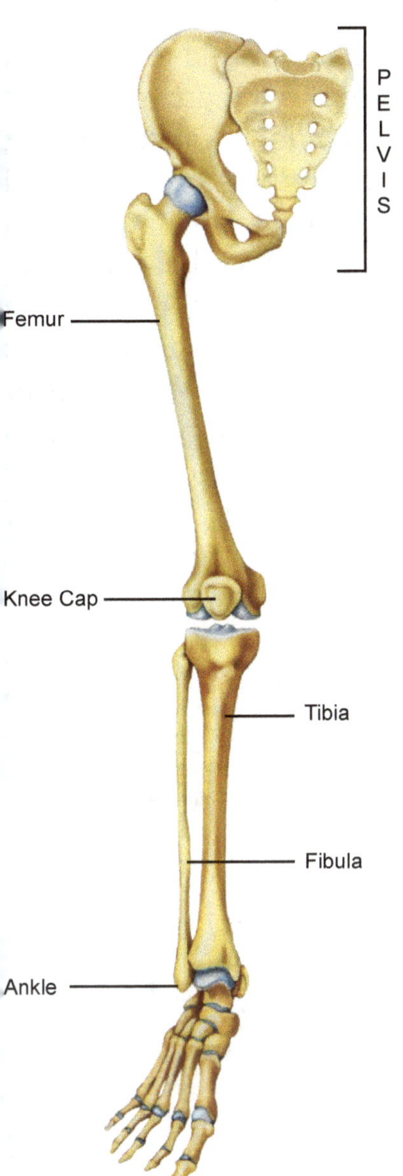

28. Foot

The foot is the base of the human leg. There are 26 bones and more than 100 muscles in the human foot. This network makes the human foot a complex part. The bones of the foot are arranged into three parts: the tarsal bones, metatarsal bones and phalanges. The metatarsal bones form the body of the foot. The phalanges create the toes. The bones of the arches of the foot are held together by ligaments (see 30 for ligaments) and are supported by muscles.

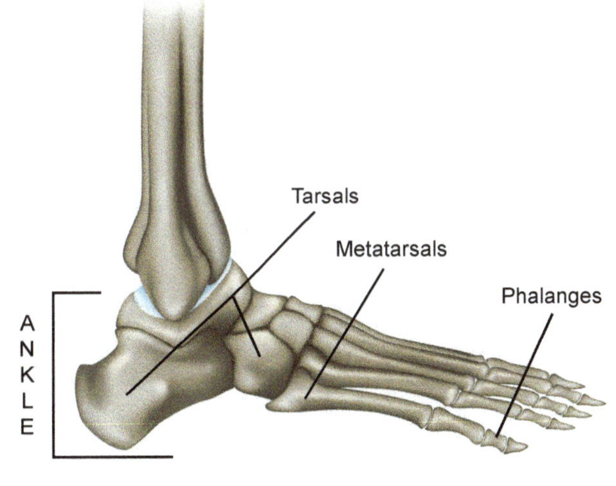

29. Joints

A joint is the place where two bones meet or the point where the bones meet the cartilage. The bones are held together at the joint by ligaments. Joints allow us to twist, turn and move our rigid skeleton. The movement of the joint is facilitated by the adjoining muscles. These muscles exert a certain degree of force on these joints which, in turn, result in a particular type of movement. There are three major classes of joints: fibrous, cartilaginous and synovial.

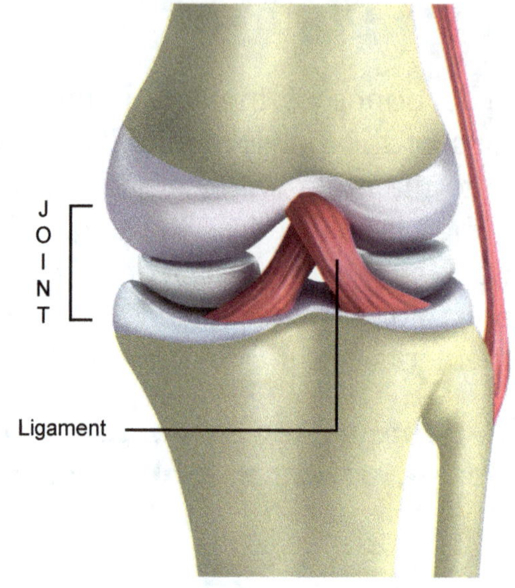

30. Ligament

A ligament is the tough band of fibrous connective tissues which provides a link to connect one bone to the other bone and form a joint. So, it can be stated that the bones are held together with the help of a ligament at the joints. A ligament provides elasticity as well as toughness to the joints. It is composed of two types of fibres: collagenous fibres and fibrocytes. Ligaments are of two types: white and yellow.

Fibrocytes

Cells that produce connective tissue proteins such as collagen.

31. Tendon

Tendon is a soft fibrous connective tissue which makes a link between the muscles and the other parts of the body, especially the bones. The main function of tendon in our body is to move the bone. The spindle-shaped fibrous tissues are called fibrocytes. The collagenous fibres present in the tendons provide them with the strength which is required for the movement of the muscles.

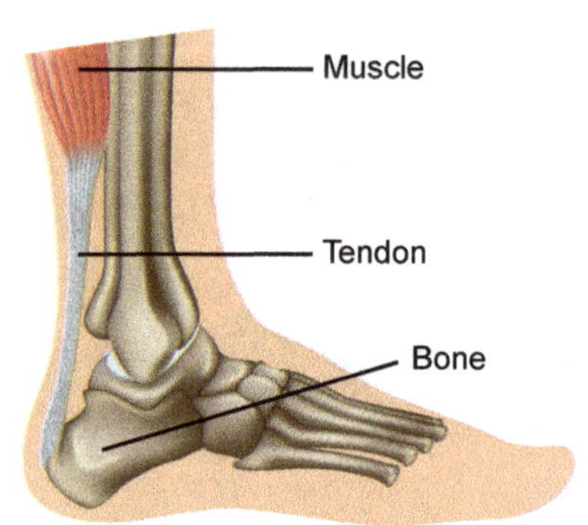

Collagenous Fibre

Part of connective tissue. It is a protein. Collagen fibres are tough and can bend, but these fibres hardly stretch.

The Achilles tendon is one of the longest tendons in the human body.

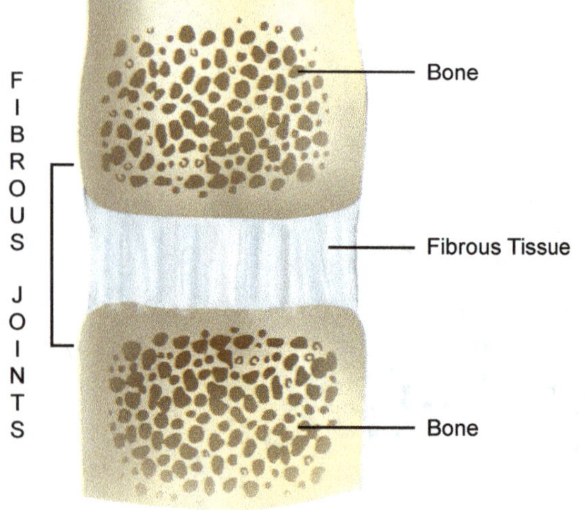

32. Fibrous joints

Fibrous joints are immovable or fixed joints in which no movement is possible. These joints are made of tough collagen fibres. Fibrous joints are found in: (1) the sutures (joints between the skull plates) of the skull; (2) the peg and socket joint found between the teeth and their bony sockets; and (3) the radio-ulnar (forearm) and the tibio-fibular (leg) joints in the upper and the lower limb, respectively.

33. Cartilaginous Joints

Cartilaginous joints are slightly movable joints in which the joint surfaces are joined by cartilages. The joints between the vertebrae in the spine and joints between the ribs are the common examples of the cartilaginous joints. The injury in the cartilage causes pain in the cartilaginous joints. The pain in the joints and stiffness is one of the classic examples of cartilage injury.

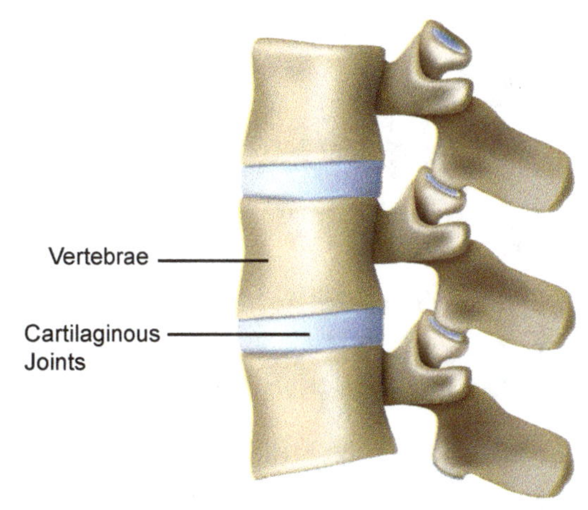

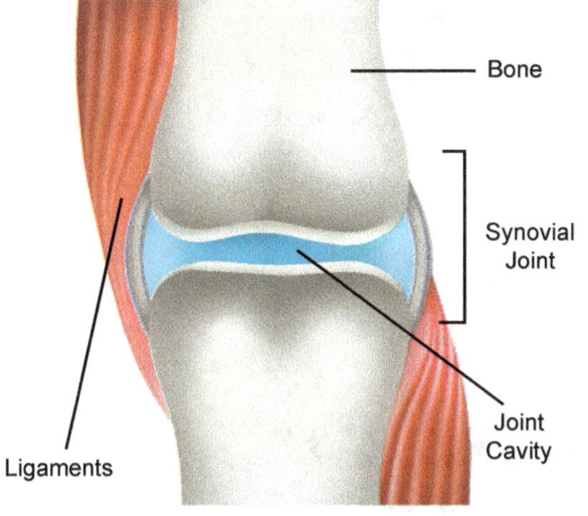

34. Synovial Joints

The synovial joints are the freely movable joints. The characteristics of a freely movable joint are: (1) the ends of bones which enter into the formation of the joints are covered by hyaline cartilage. (2) Ligaments are required to bind the bones together. (3) There is a joint cavity that is enclosed by a capsule of fibrous tissue. The synovial capsule reduces the friction between the bones allowing more smooth movement. This type of joints is present in the elbow, knee, shoulder and hip joint, etc.

35. Ball and Socket Joint

The ball and socket joint or sphere-shaped joint is a joint in which one of the bones is round like a ball. The round bone fits into another bone which resembles a socket. The round bone rotates within the socket bone. This type of joint permits the bone to move in all directions. The two shoulder joints and the two hip joints are the common examples of ball and socket joints.

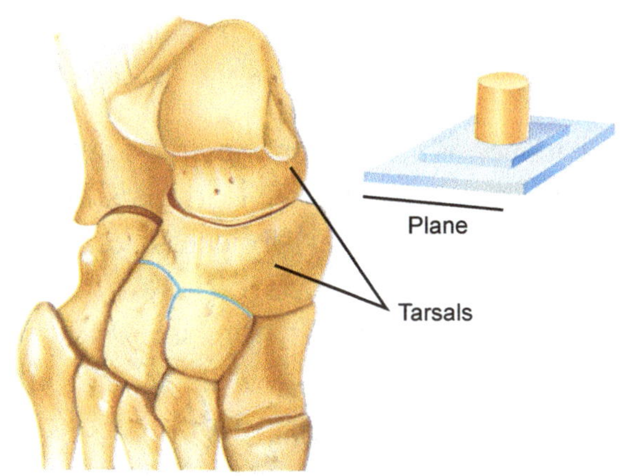

36. Gliding Joint

A gliding joint is also referred as a plane or planar joint in which two flat surfaces of a bone move smoothly on each other. In this type of joint, the connecting surfaces of the involved bones are flat or slightly curved. These joints allow only gliding movement. These are found between the carpal bones of the wrist; carpals and the metacarpals of the palm; tarsal bones of the ankle; and tarsals and the metatarsals of the foot.

Gliding Movement

Movement on a surface, such as sliding over a surface or a twisting movement.

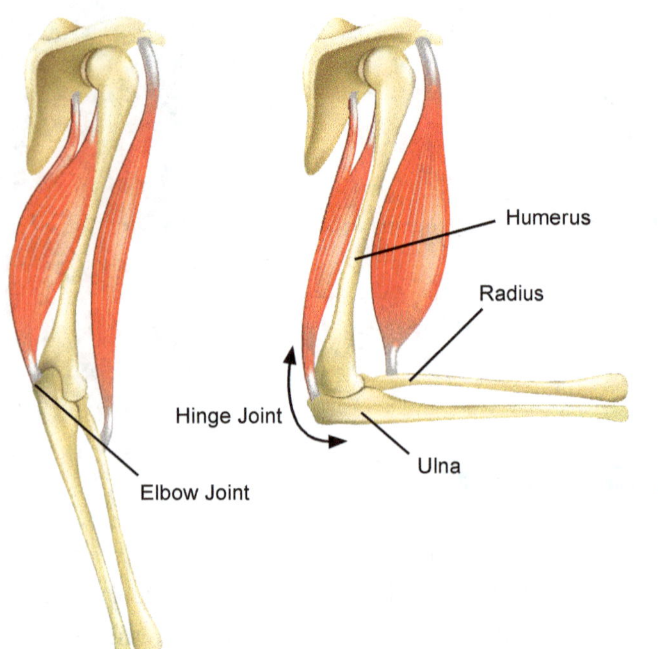

37. Hinge Joint

The other class of synovial joints are the hinge joints. A hinge joint works like a hinge fixed to a door or window. A hinge joint allows bones to move in one direction, that is only a backward and a forward motion. In the human body, we can find the hinge joints between the bones of the fingers (phalanges) and between the inner bone of the forearm and the humerus at the elbow. The synovial membrane secretes lubricant to keep these joints lubricated.

38. Pivot Joint

In a pivot joint, one bone moves without disturbing other bones. This joint is found between the head and the neck. This joint is also called the rotatory joint that allows only rotational movement, as in case of the movement of the head. One can turn one's head from right to left or from left to right because of this joint.

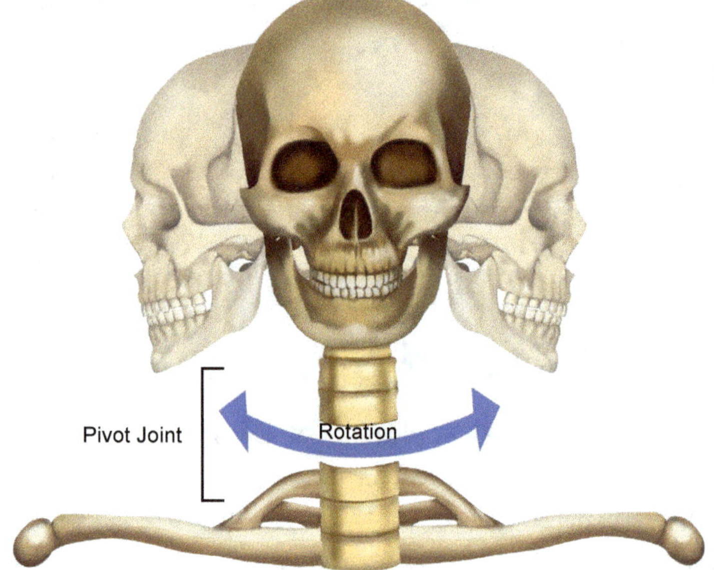

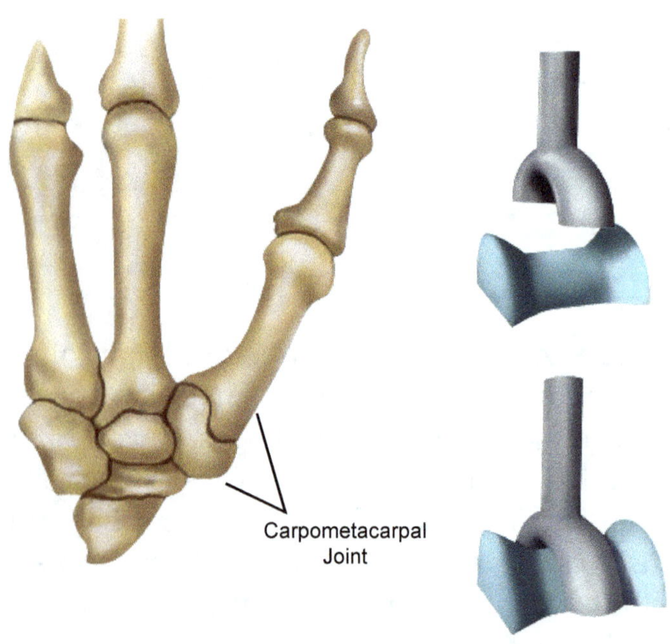

39. Saddle Joint

A saddle joint has an interesting arrangement of bones in it. In this joint, one bone is shaped like a saddle with the other bone resting on it like a rider on a horse. These joints are much balanced and stable joints as compared to the hinge joint. The best example of a saddle joint in the body is the carpometacarpal joint of the thumb that is formed between the second trapezium-shaped bone and the first metacarpal.

40. Muscular System

The muscular system is mainly responsible for the movement of the body. The muscles help carry out everyday activities such as walking and sitting. This system supports maintenance of the posture and stability of the joints. The muscles in the body help generate heat necessary for various metabolic functions. There are more than six hundred muscles in the human body. The muscles are of three types: the cardiac, the skeletal and the smooth muscles. Each type of muscle performs a specific function.

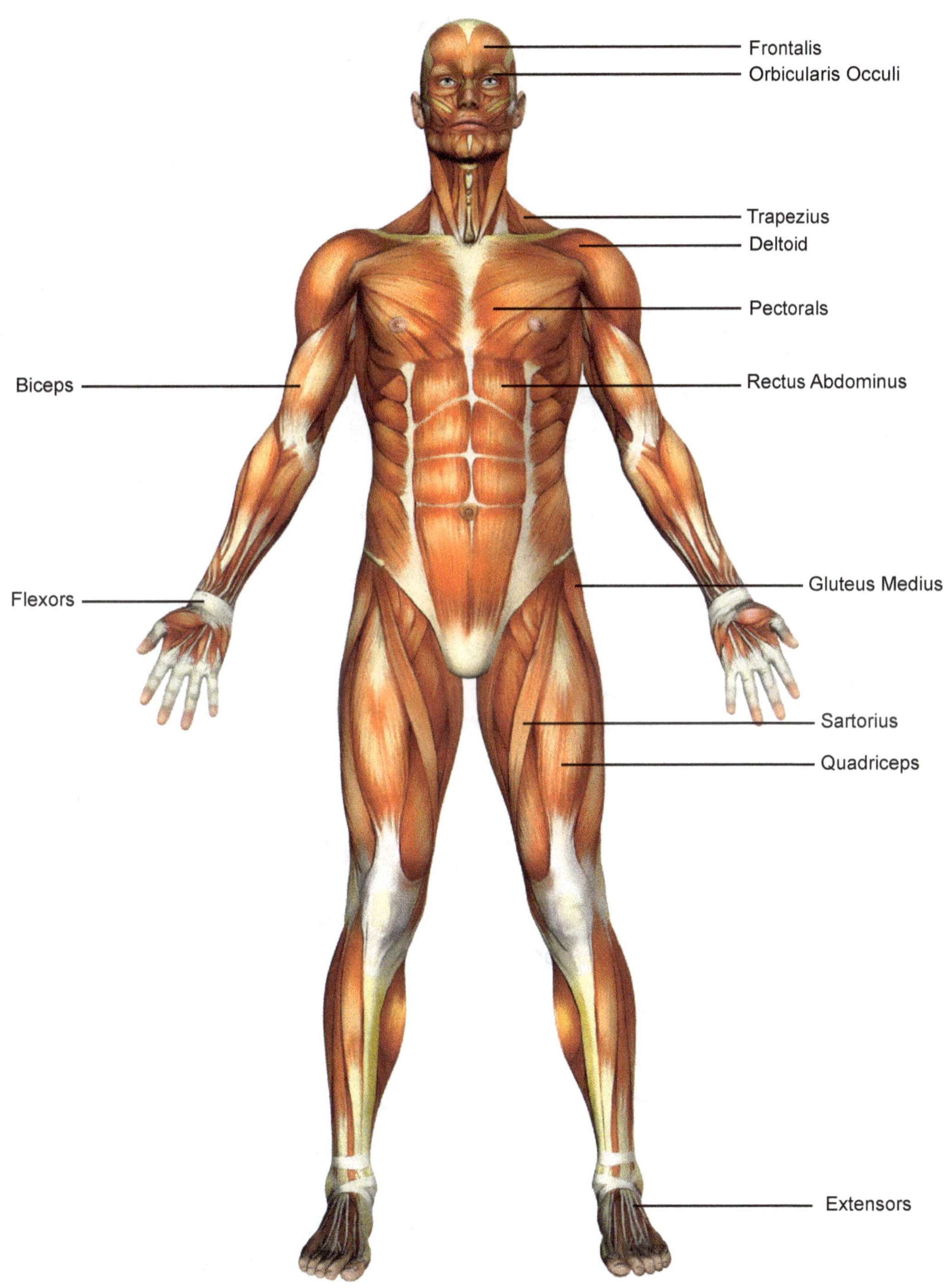

Muscles are also categorised as 'lifting' muscle and 'lowering' muscle on the basis of the movement they support.

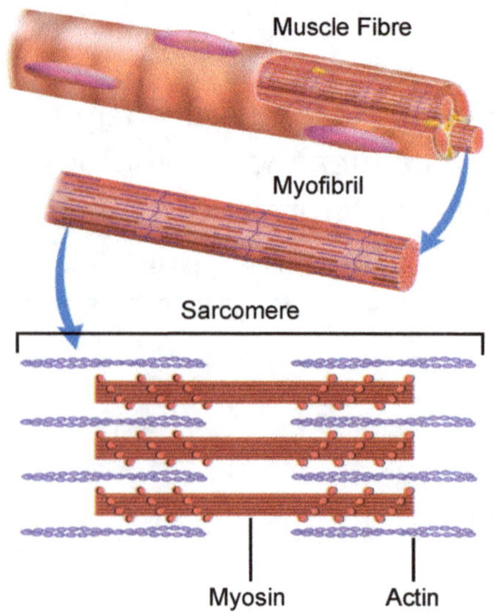

41. Muscle Fibre

Muscles consist of several muscle bundles. These muscle bundles are composed of several muscle fibres or myocytes. They are held together by a layer of connective tissue and are lined by sarcolemma. Each muscle fibre is composed of several parallely arranged strands called myofibrils. The myofibrils contain two important proteins: actin and myosin. The striated appearance of the muscle fibre is due to these proteins. Actin forms the light band and myosin forms the dark band.

42. Cardiac Muscle

Cardiac muscle is a unique type of muscle that is found only in the heart. These muscles are formed by specialised muscle tissues, composed of striated cells. These cells help the heart to pump the blood to the entire body. The pumping of blood is possible due to the contraction of the heart muscles. These muscle contractions are controlled by the brain. The human brain releases specific chemicals that adjust the rate of muscle contraction.

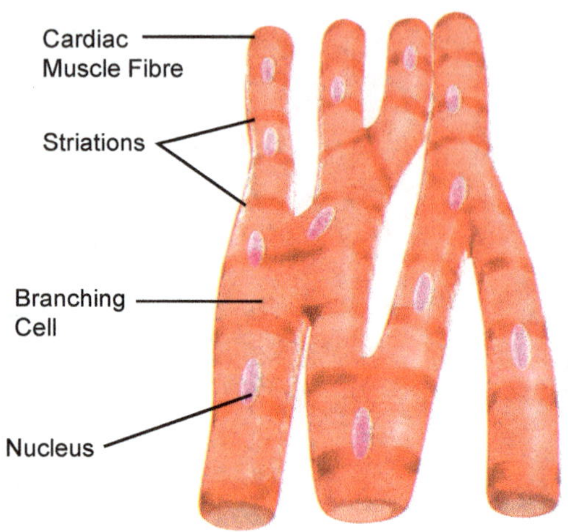

Exercising strengthens our muscles, especially the heart muscles and maintains a good blood flow throughout the body.

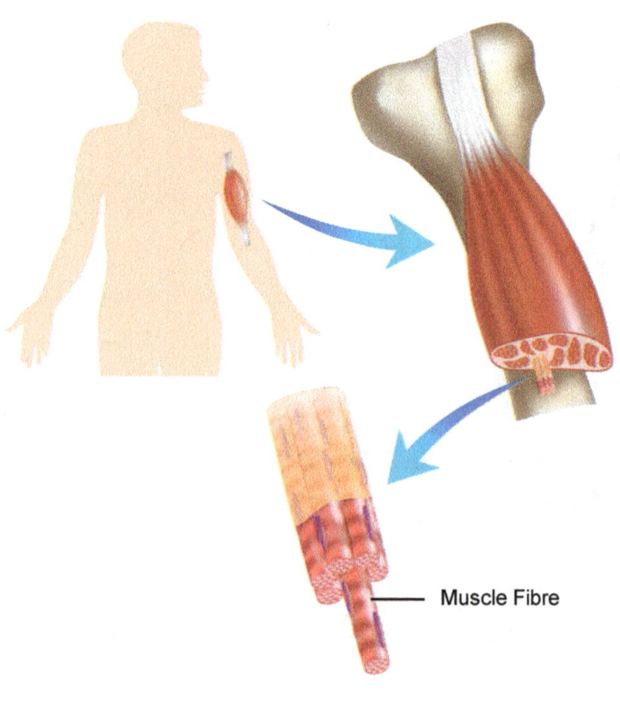

43. Skeletal Muscle

Skeletal muscles are the only voluntary muscles in the body. These muscles are connected with the skeleton, hence are called skeletal muscles. These muscles are composed of striated muscle tissues. Somatic nervous system is responsible for every action of these muscles. This is the reason why these are called voluntary muscles. These muscles are usually attached to two definite bones by the tendons. Skeletal muscles create contraction force to move the body-parts which are closer to the bone, that are attached to the muscle.

Voluntary Muscles

The muscles whose movement can be controlled by an individual's own will.

44. Smooth Muscle

Smooth muscles are also called visceral muscles as they are present in the internal organs of the body, such as blood vessels, the gastrointestinal tract, the bladder or the uterus. These muscles are responsible for the contraction/movement of the internal organs. The smooth muscles are the weakest muscles and are controlled by the brain. The cell size of the smooth muscle is small. They greatly differ from the skeletal muscles as they are smooth, uniform and they have no striations.

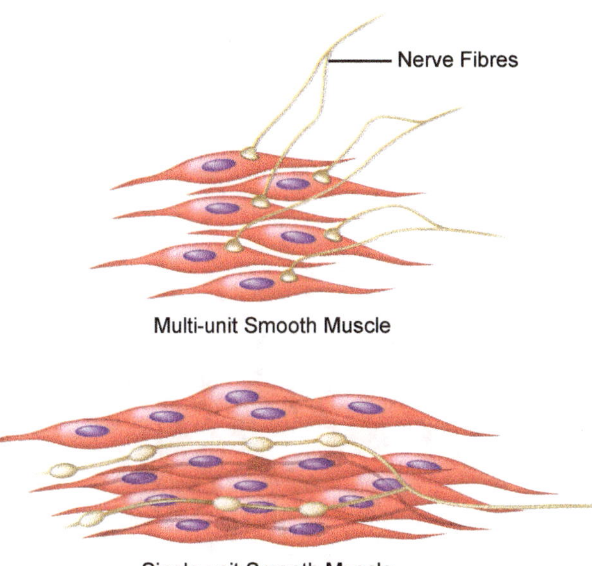

Viscera

The internal body organs

45. Epicranius Muscles

The muscles that cover the skull are the epicranius muscles. The epicranius muscles are comprised of two muscles: the frontalis muscle and the occipitalis muscle. The muscle located on the forehead is the frontalis muscle, while the occipitalis muscle is located on the right and the left side of the skull on the back side. These two muscles work together to lift the eyebrows and wrinkle the forehead. The frontalis muscle is a thin muscle, which is of quadrilateral form.

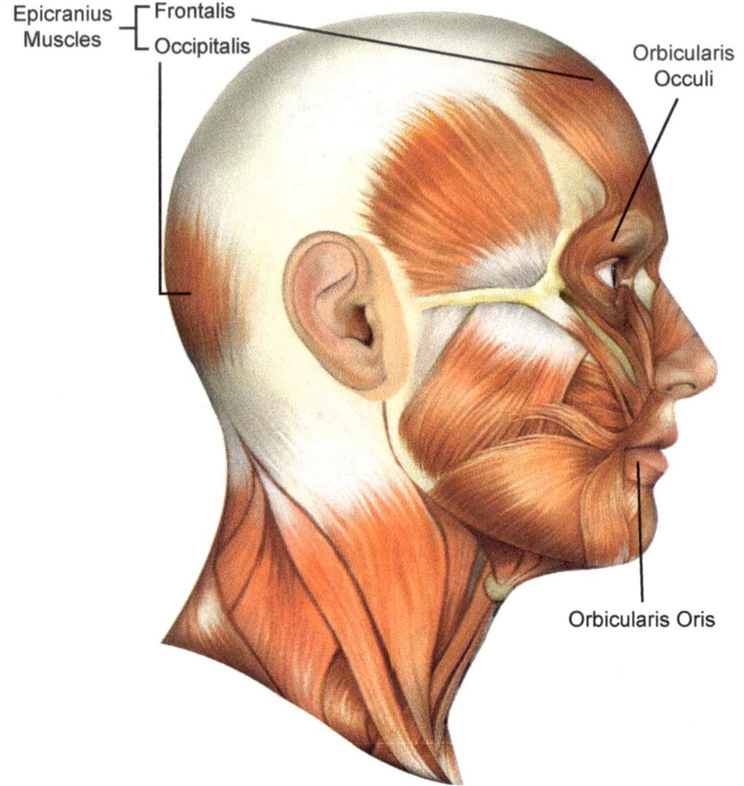

46. Orbicularis Occuli

The orbicularis occuli muscle is the facial muscle that surrounds the eyelids. Externally, it looks like a ring-like band. It is made up of skeletal muscle fibres. The main function of this muscle is to help the eye to blink. Along with this, these muscles also provide a definite shape to the eye and help in the compression of the tear gland, thus facilitating the flow of tears.

47. Orbicularis Oris

The orbicularis oris muscle encircles the mouth. It provides a definite shape to the lips. These muscles are located between the skin and mucous membrane of the lips. These muscles control the movements originating in the jaw bones of the mouth. They also facilitate various facial expressions and help us to play various musical instruments such as flute, mouth organ, etc.

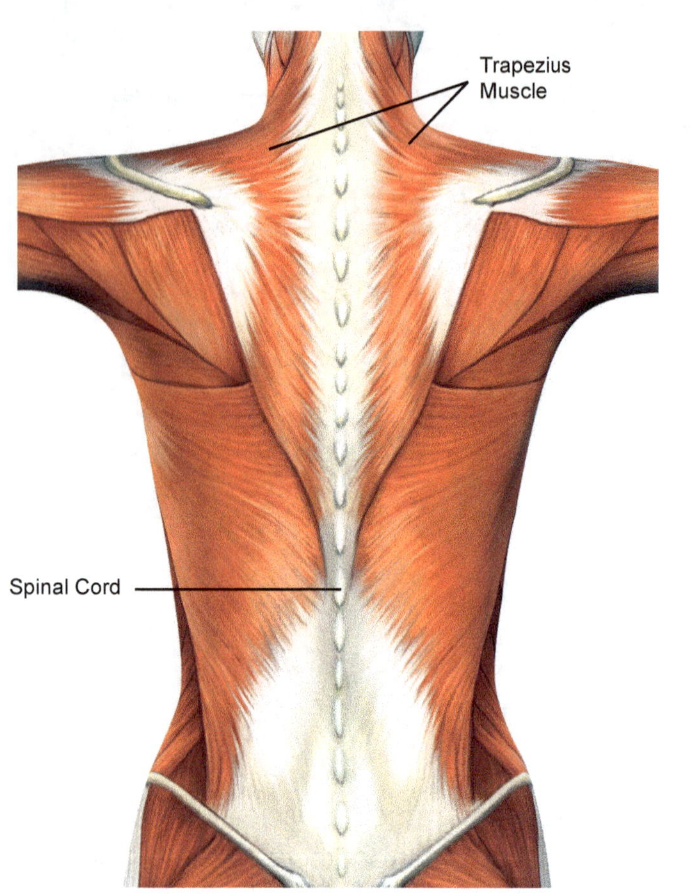

48. Trapezius Muscle

Trapezius muscle is found in the upper and back portion of the neck, shoulders and chest. This is one of the vital muscles of the upper part of the back. It is a large triangular muscle. It extends from the uppermost point of the neck to the spine and the shoulder blade region. The main functions of this muscle are to provide support to the shoulder, and limbs and help in the movement and rotation of the neck.

Shoulder Blade

A bone that connects the upper arm bone to the collar bone

49. Deltoid Muscle

Deltoid muscle is found on the uppermost part of the arm. It covers the top of the shoulder joint. It resembles an equilateral triangle in shape. This muscle helps in the movement and rotation of the neck and mainly it provides stability to the shoulder blade. It helps in the lifting and twisting of the arm.

50. Pectorals

The pectorals are located on the chest. There are two types of pectoral muscles: the pectoralis major and the pectoralis minor. They create the bulk of the chest and are known as pecs. They extend from the shoulder to the breast bone. The contractions of the pectoralis major pull the upper arm bone and result in the lateral, vertical or rotational motion. The pectoralis minor muscle is located below the pectoralis major muscle. The pectorals control the movement of the arm and also help the chest muscles during deep breathing.

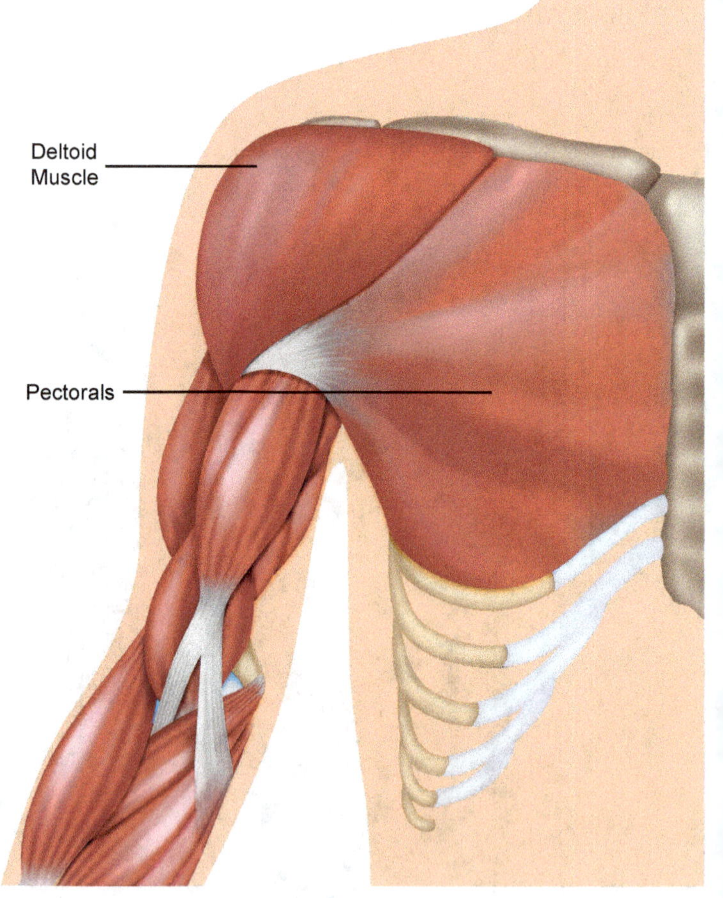

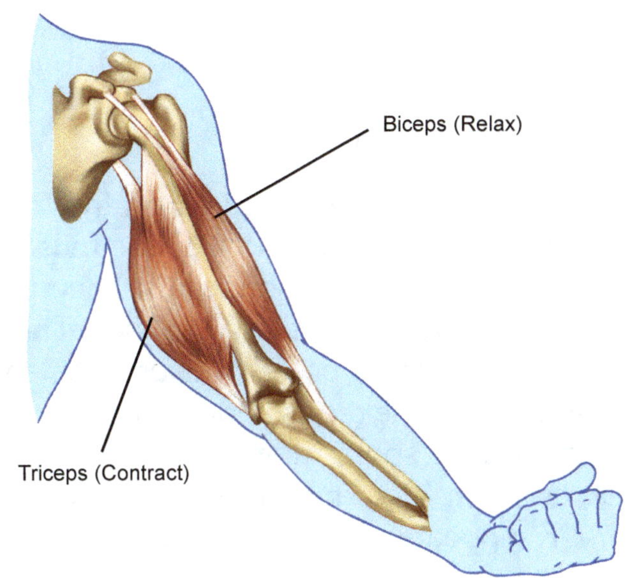

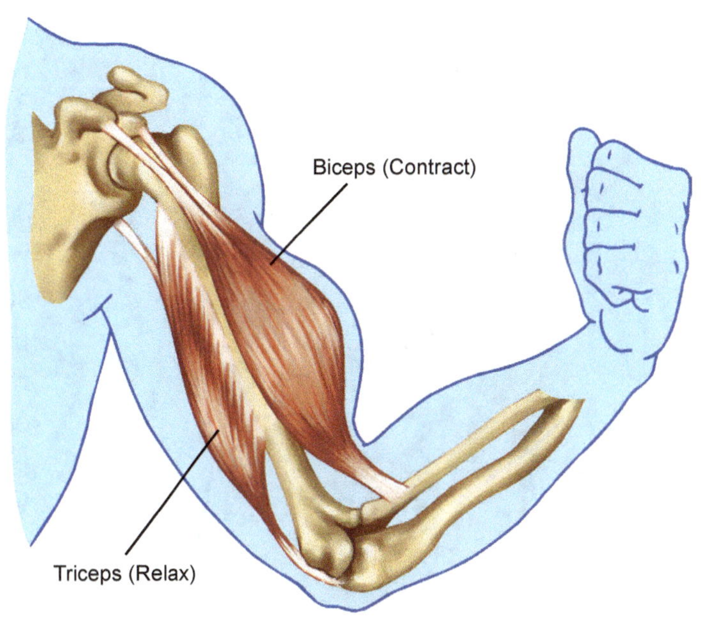

51. Biceps

The biceps are two-headed muscles on the front part of the upper arm. They are divided into two parts: the long head and the short head. They are one of the skeletal muscles that help in the movement of the elbow and the shoulder. While lifting the load, the motion of the shoulder and the elbow joints is controlled by the biceps. The biceps pull the bones near the elbow when we raise our forearm.

Muscle Contraction

It takes place when we move or we try to push or pull an object. During muscle contraction, the muscle fibres (the light and dark myofibrils) slide over one another and when the muscle is relaxed, after the performance of the movement, the same muscle fibres slide apart. The moment we perform a movement, the skin covering the muscles stretches and the muscles flex.

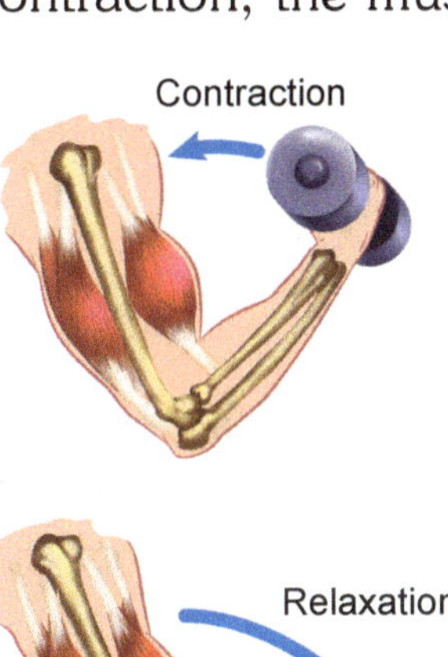

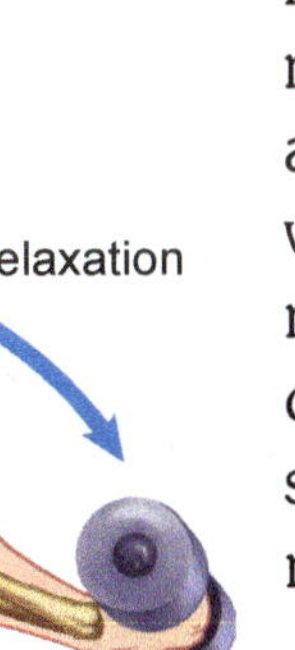

52. Triceps

The triceps are located in the upper arm of the human body. They travel down between the shoulder and the elbow along the humerus, the long bone in the arm. In association with biceps, they facilitate extension and contraction of the forearm. The biceps and the triceps work in association. The main function of the triceps is the extension of the elbow joint which results in the straightening of the arm. The triceps and the biceps are the opponent of each other.

When the muscles involuntarily contract for a longer period, we experience spasm. During a spasm, we feel a slight tightness or a knot in a muscle. Spasms are experienced by athletes when they perform strenuous activities. Spasms are also referred as cramps. Generally, cramps are temporary and cause sudden pain, but some cramps, if persist for a longer time, may cause tendon or ligament injury.

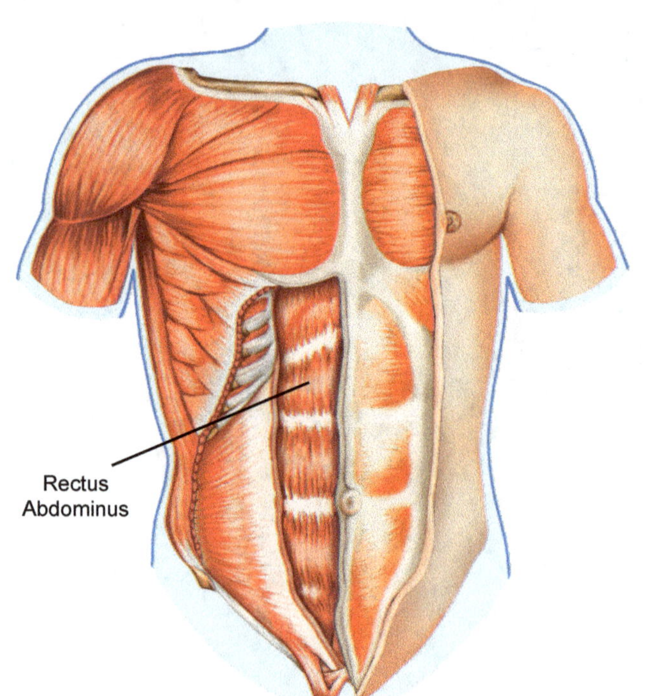

Rectus Abdominus

53. Rectus Abdominus

The rectus abdominus muscle is located on the front part of the body in the abdominal region. These muscles support the forward bending of the back, and they pull the ribs and the pelvis inwards and curve the back. These muscles are also used during bowel movements and coughing. Strengthening of the rectus abdominus muscles improves performance in sports that require jumping. When the fat layers from these muscles are removed, a classical 'SIX-PACK' appearance can be viewed on these muscles.

54. Wrist and Finger Flexors

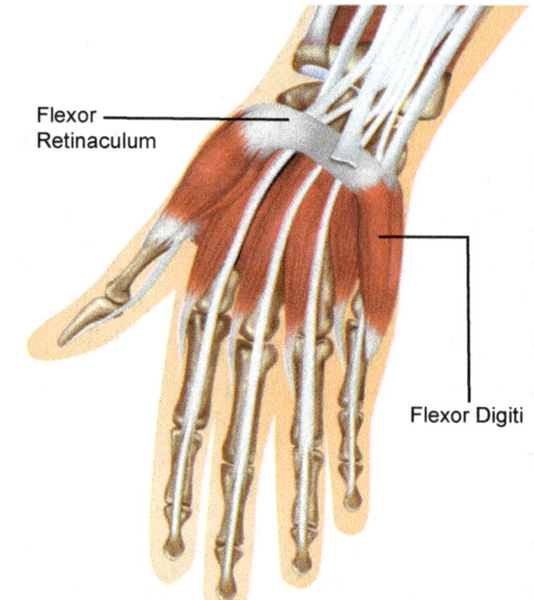

Flexors are the muscles that flex a joint. A wrist and the adjoining fingers have multiple muscles that work together to bring about complex movements. Flexor muscles are found at the front side of the forearm. Flexor muscles help flex the wrist. A few of them are: flexor digiti, flexor retinaculum, etc. These muscles emerge from the humerus of the upper arm. The main function of wrist flexors is to bend the wrist towards the arm, while that of the finger flexors is to make a fist.

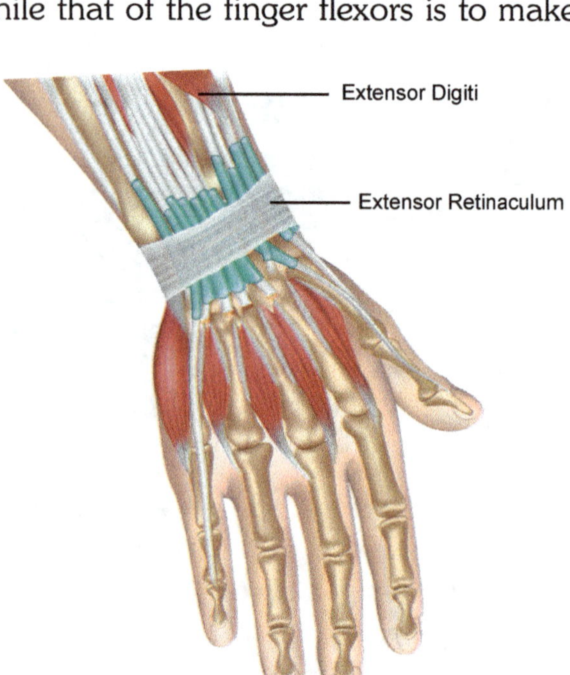

55. Wrist and Finger Extensors

Extensor muscles, as the name suggests, are the muscles which help extend the joints or stretch the joints. The wrist extensors are located at the back side of the lower arm. These muscles support the palm to move away from the arm. The extensor muscles help extend the hand at the wrist. A few of them are: extensor digiti, extensor retinaculum, etc.

56. Muscles of Leg

There are different types of muscles in the leg. They are: quadriceps femoris, iliopsoas and sartorius in the front and the hamstrings and gluteus maximus at the back. These muscles at the front help bend the thigh, extending the leg at the knee, while those in the back help extend the thigh at the hip and bend the leg at the knee. All the leg muscles help maintain the proper posture and balance of the body.

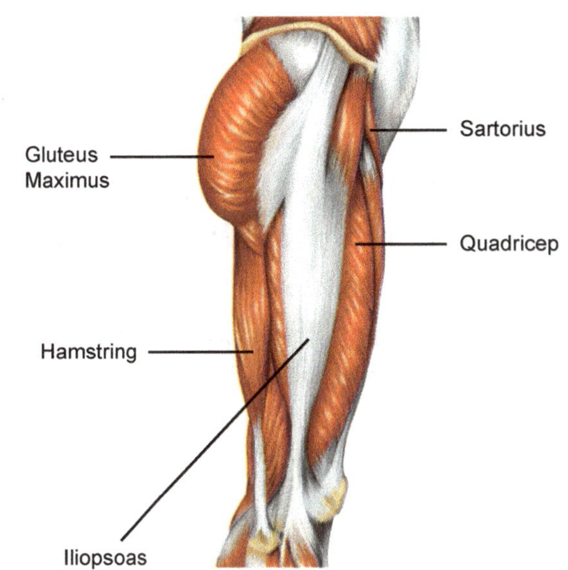

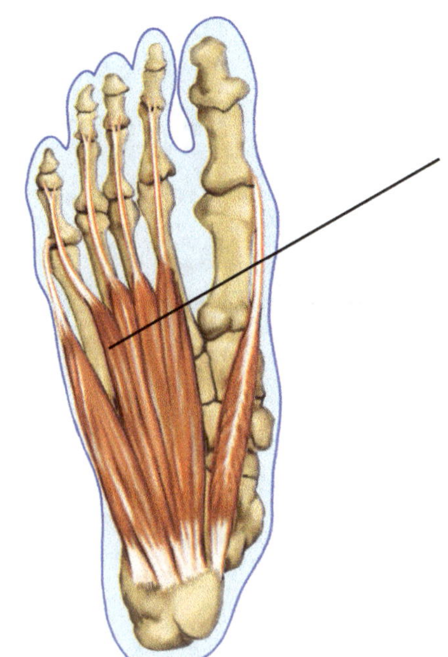

57. Muscles of Foot and Toe

The muscles located at the lower side of the knee are responsible for the movement of the ankle, foot and toes. The foot muscles can be classified into two types: extrinsic and intrinsic muscles. These muscles originate on the frontal or back sides of the lower leg, and on the top or base sides of the foot, respectively. The flexor digitorum brevis and its associated extensor muscles are responsible for the toe movement.

Food, Muscle Building and Sports

Food rich in protein helps in body building, especially muscles. Sportspersons need extra calories (additional 500 calories) in their daily diet to build up their muscles. An increase in calorie intake from all the three macro nutrients (carbohydrates, proteins and fats), allows optimum usage of protein for muscle building in the body. If sportsperson do not consume enough calories, the muscle gain is limited.

Studies say that when carbohydrate and protein-rich diet is consumed within 30 minutes of a workout, the amino acid and carbohydrate stores of the muscles are replenished. Amino acids are the building blocks of the protein and a diet rich in protein helps promote muscular growth and recovery. Carbohydrate is another equally important macro nutrient required during training. The energy released by the break-down of carbohydrates helps generate necessary fuel for tough training. The important food options are: meat, poultry, fish, dairy products, eggs, nuts, and dried beans. Foods like turkey sandwiches, crackers and cheese, or an energy bar containing 7 to 14 grams of protein are good choices.

58. Circulatory System

The circulatory system is human body's transport system. The system consists of the heart, blood vessels and lymphatics. The circulatory system is responsible for:

(a) Transport of nutrients and oxygen to the cells;

(b) Transport of carbon dioxide and other waste products of cellular respiration; and

(c) Circulation of hormones and chemical components and maintenance of the body temperature.

The heart is the central organ of the circulatory system; it pumps blood throughout the body. The heart is connected with blood vessels. These are tube-like organs that carry the blood. The third component of this system is the lymphatics that collect and filter the blood.

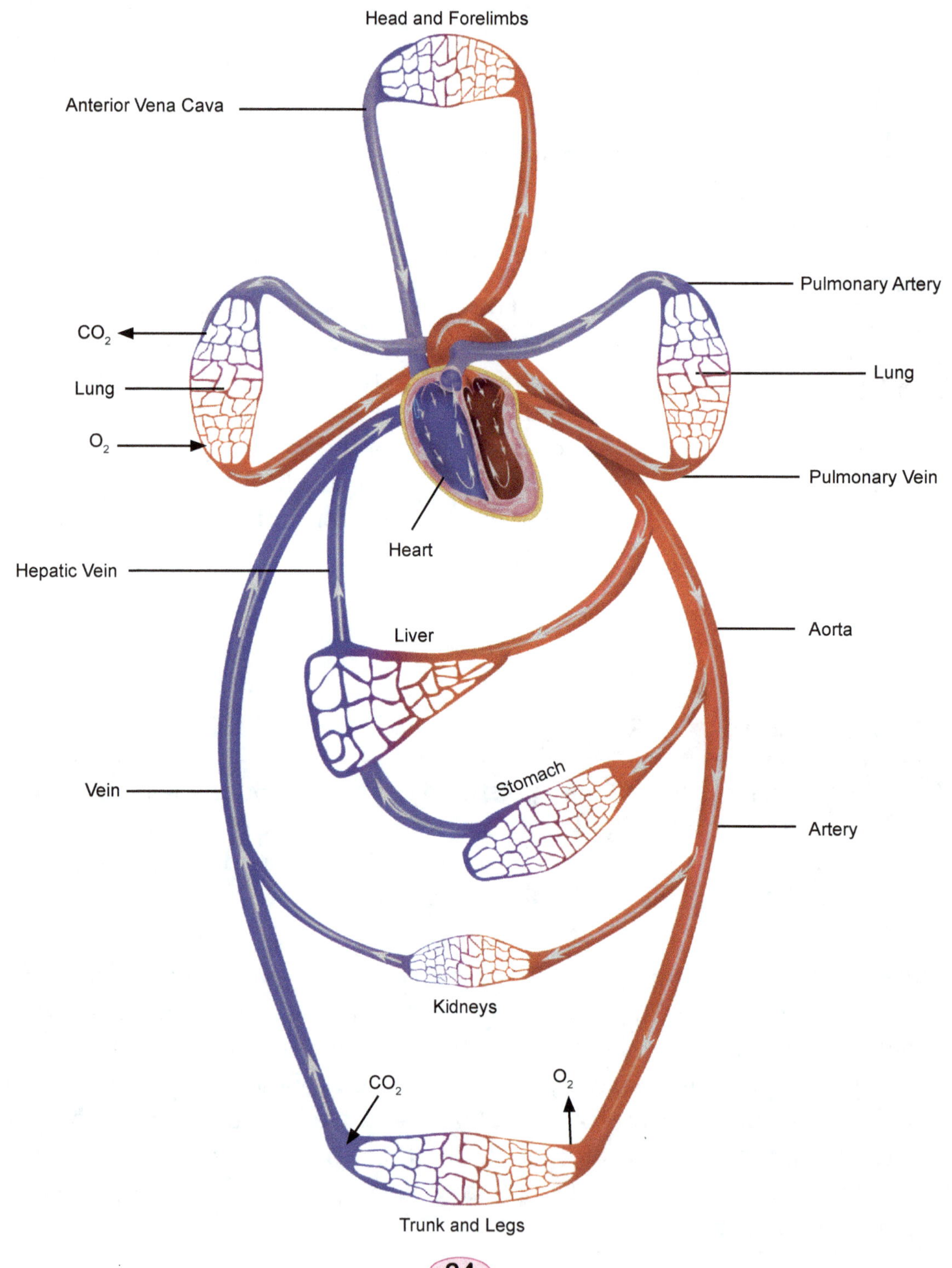

59. Blood

Blood is a fluid tissue composed of two parts: liquid and solid. Plasma is the liquid part, and blood cells like red blood cells and white blood cells are the solid part of the blood. Blood cells float in plasma. Plasma is a straw-coloured liquid. Blood cells are made in the bone marrow. Blood carries oxygen to the body tissues. The oxygen carried by the blood is bound to haemoglobin, an iron containing protein. Blood also transports salts and carbon dioxide. It can be said that blood is a vehicle that runs throughout the body.

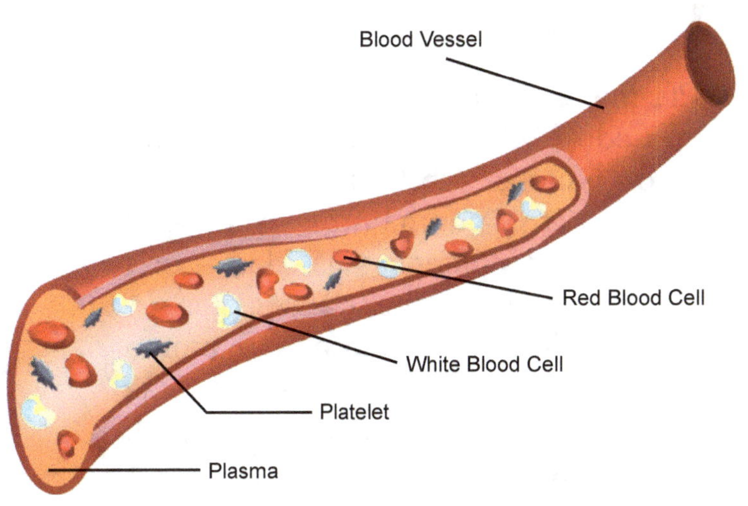

Blood cells are formed in bone marrow, lymph nodes, tonsils and spleen.

Red Blood Cells (Erythrocytes)

White Blood Cells (Leucocytes)

Platelets (Thrombocytes)

60. Red Blood Cells

The red blood cells (RBCs) are also called erythrocytes, which are spherical in shape with a depression in the middle to impart maximum surface area to the cells. The greater the surface area the more they are able to capture oxygen. RBCs get their red colour from oxygenated iron-rich protein haemoglobin. Hence the arteries are depicted by red colour. Haemoglobin is a pigment that binds oxygen and forms oxyhaemoglobin. These cells have an average life of about 120 days.

Bone marrow is a soft spongy, either red or yellow-coloured, tissue that fills the gaps inside the bones. It is also called the myeloid.

61. White Blood Cells

White blood cells (WBCs or leucocytes) are the transparent and colourless cells. They are larger in size and fewer in number than red cells. The main function of the white cells is producing antibodies to defend the body against infection and disease. The white cells are referred as the soldier's body. The count of WBCs increases when there is an infection in the human body. These cells have amoeba-like movement, due to which these cells can reach the infected parts of the body.

62. Thrombocytes

The thrombocytes or blood platelets are the smallest cells in the body, about one-third size of the red blood cells. Thrombocytes play an important role in the clotting of blood and control of bleeding after injury. In case of injury, these platelets gather in large numbers immediately and plug the injured cavity by attaching at the site and to one another. Platelets occupy a much smaller fraction of the volume of the blood.

63. Plasma

Plasma is a straw-coloured fluid. It is composed of 90% of water and less than 10% of various substances in solution which consists of plasma proteins, organic substances and inorganic salts. Plasma acts as the medium for the transmission of nutrients, salts, fats, glucose and amino acids to the tissues. It also acts as the medium for carrying away waste material, such as urea, uric acid and carbon dioxide.

The patients of cancer and leukaemia need plasma transfusions.

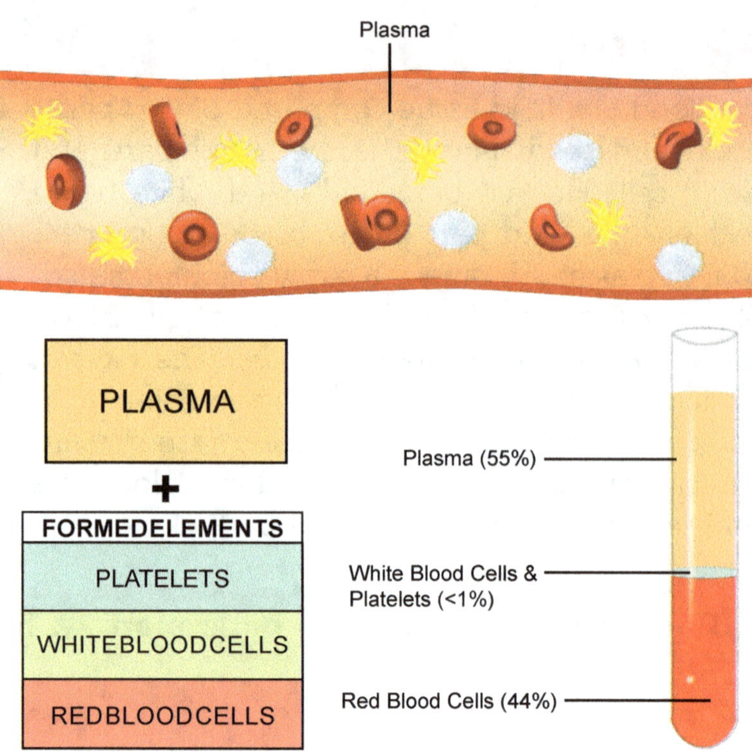

64. Heart

The heart is a hollow, cone-shaped, muscular organ. It is a biological pump. Its size is not more than a human's clenched fist and is made up of specialised cardiac muscles. The heart lies at the centre of the chest cavity, between the lungs and behind the sternum. It is slightly tilted towards the left. The heart has four chambers, which are separated by septum, a wall of muscles. Two upper chambers are called atria and two lower chambers are called ventricles. The valves in the heart are specialised to ensure unidirectional flow of blood.

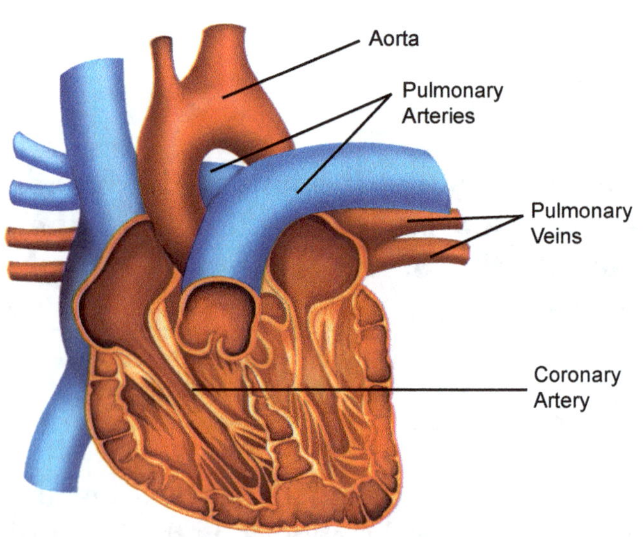

Cross-sectional View

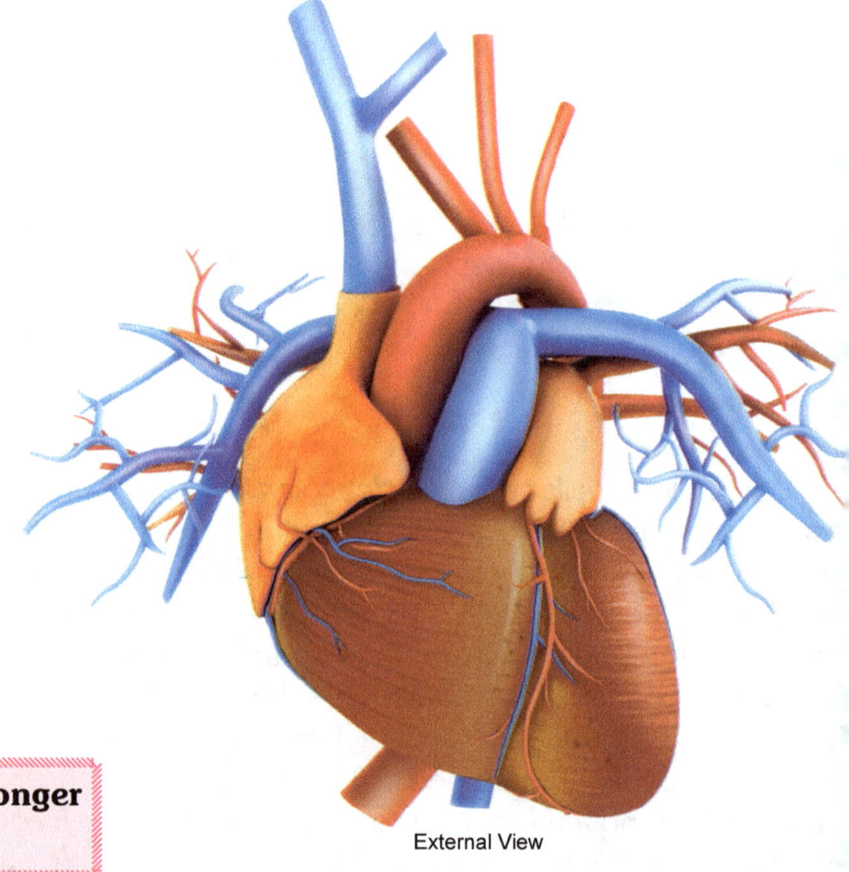

External View

The left ventricle of the heart has stronger muscles than the right one.

65. Blood Vessel

There is a network of tubes in the human body to circulate blood. This network of tubes is called blood vessels. Blood vessels are thin tubes that are attached to the heart. They are the roads on which the blood as a vehicle flows. The three major types of vessels are arteries, veins and capillaries. They all have different functions in the blood circulation process.

Arteries transfer blood away from the heart, veins transfer blood towards the heart and capillaries form a capillary lake by uniting the arteries and the veins.

Arterioles & Venules

Arterioles are tiny branches of arteries that lead to capillaries.

Venules are minute vessels that drain blood from capillaries and into veins.

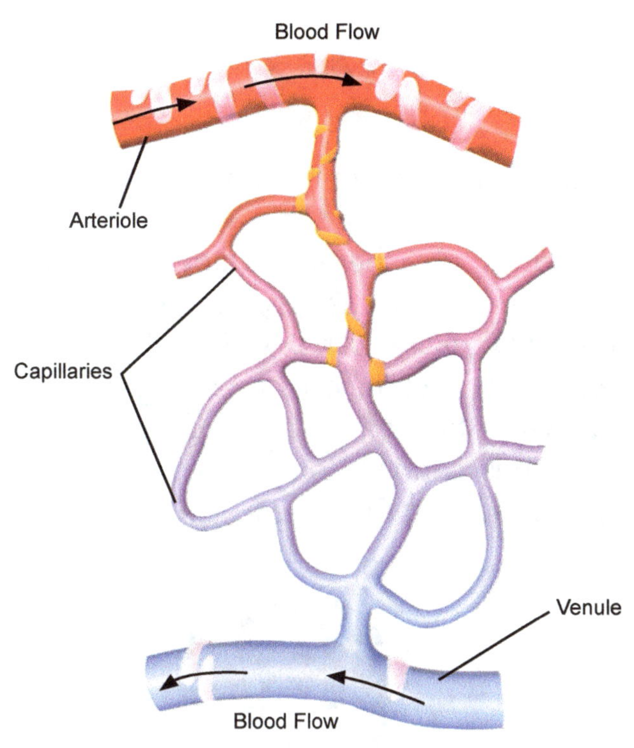

66. Artery

Arteries are the blood vessels that transfer oxygenated blood from the heart to all the parts of the body, except pulmonary artery, which carries deoxygenated blood. Arteries have thick elastic walls to bear the high pressure of blood, as the heart pumps blood into the arteries. Arteries divide into smaller vessels called arterioles, which link up with capillaries in the capillary network. To feel the blood rushing through the arteries we can place two fingers in the hollow spot on the wrist.

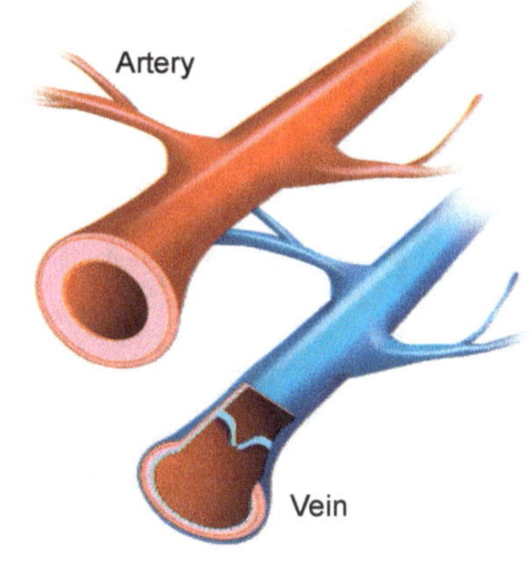

67. Vein

Veins are the blood vessels that transfer deoxygenated blood from the various parts of the body back to the heart after it has delivered oxygen to the body. Pulmonary vein is the only vein which carries pure blood. Veins are located much nearer to the surface of the body than arteries. Veins and venules (tiny veins that link up with capillaries and drain blood from them) bear very low blood pressures. Hence, veins have much thinner, less elastic and less muscular walls than the walls of arteries.

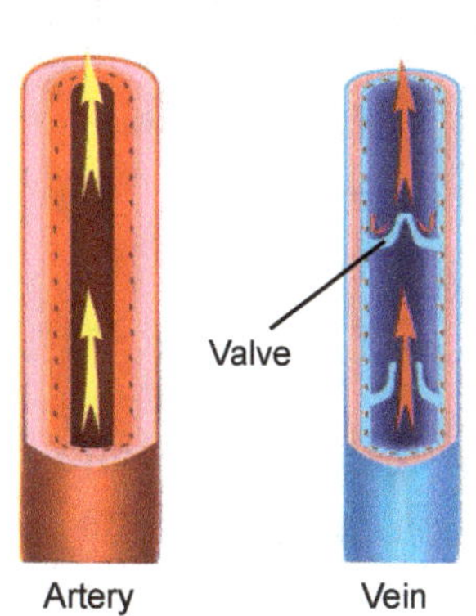

The veins of the body builders are slightly inflated and they show up prominently on their skin as they carry a huge volume of deoxygenated blood from the muscles to the heart.

68. Capillaries

Capillaries are the thinnest blood vessels, composed of ultra thin layer of tissues. Capillaries are the important link between arteries and veins, as they transfer blood from arteries to veins. The wall of the capillary permits an exchange of food material, gases and waste between the blood and the cells. Capillaries connect to arterioles on one end and venules on the other.

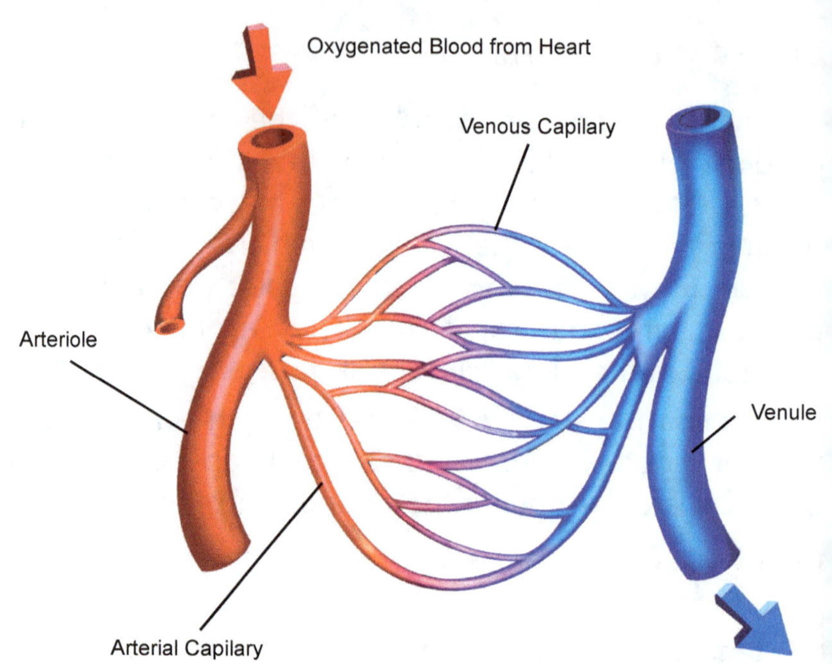

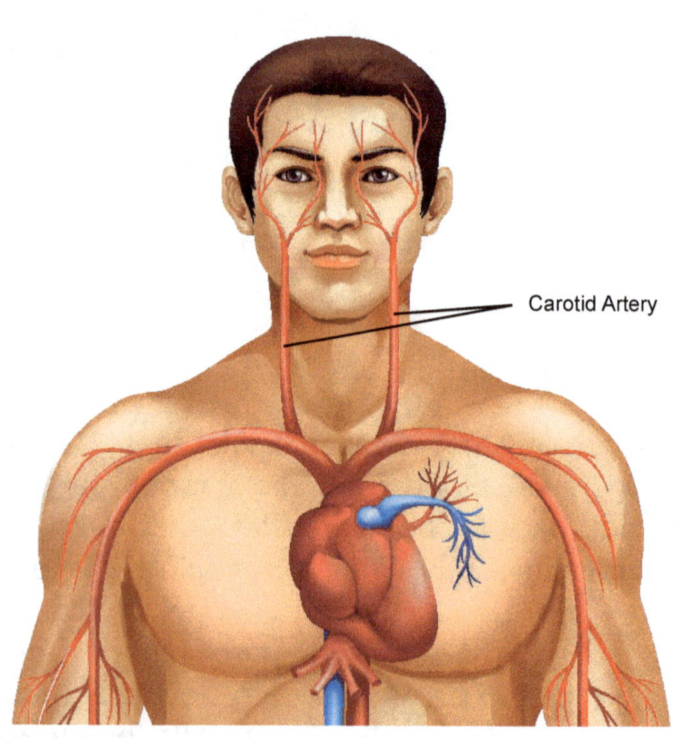

69. Carotid Arteries

There are two carotid arteries, located at the front part of the neck. The carotid arteries are the major arteries of the human body. These arteries supply oxygenated blood to the front part of the brain. There are two carotid arteries: one lies on the right side and other lies on the left side of the neck. Each carotid artery of the neck then branches into two divisions: internal and external carotid arteries. The internal carotid artery supplies blood to the brain and the external supplies blood to the face and the neck.

70. Jugular Vein

Jugular vein is a set of four large veins that send back deoxygenated blood from the head and neck to the heart. There are two types of jugular veins: external and internal jugulars. These are located on each side of the neck. The internal jugular lies deep in the neck. It contains blood which has drained from the front part of the skull. The external jugular vein is the superficial vein. The internal jugular veins are much larger than the external ones.

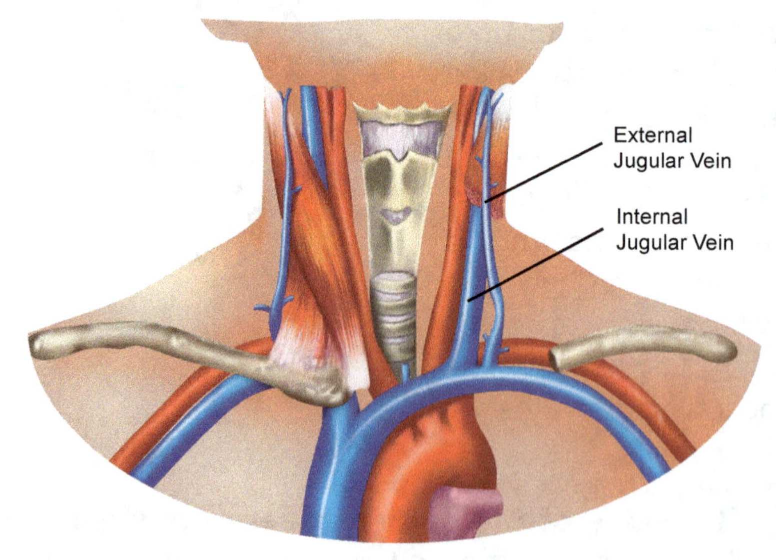

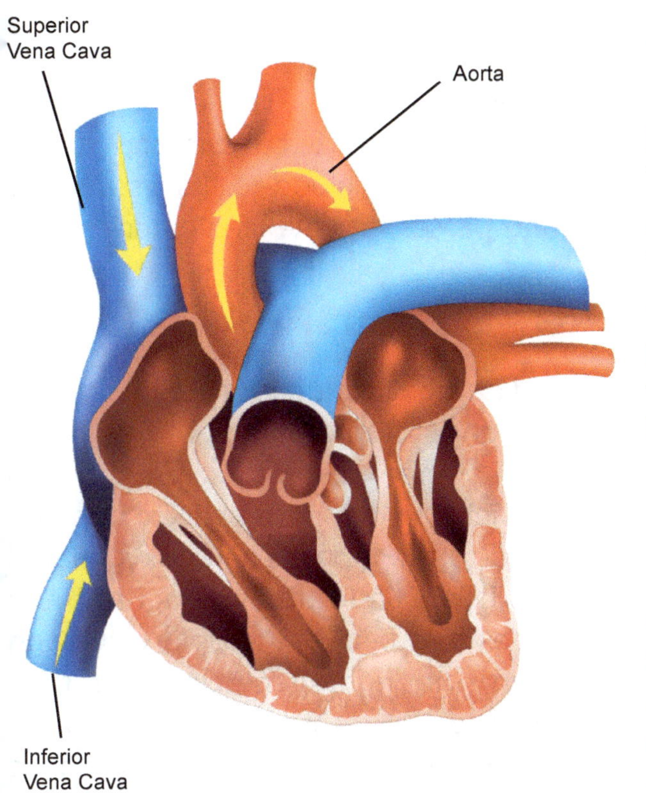

71. Superior Vena Cava

Superior vena cava is also referred as precava. It is a large vein, but short in length, located above the heart. The venae cavae are the largest veins in the body. They carry deoxygenated blood to the right atrium of the heart. There is no valve between the superior vena cava and the right atrium of the heart. The blood flowing from the precava to the heart causes contraction of the heart. This vein is formed by the veins which return deoxygenated blood from the upper limbs, neck and head to the heart.

72. Inferior Vena Cava

Inferior vena cava is also known as the posterior vena cava. It is the second largest vein of the heart, located at the lower part of the heart. Inferior vena cava carries deoxygenated blood from the parts of the body lying in the abdominal region to the heart. The inferior vena cava also drains the deoxygenated blood into the right atrium. Two major leg veins, iliac veins form the inferior vena cava.

73. Aorta

Aorta is the largest and the main artery of the body that supplies oxygenated blood to the body system. It looks like a tube that is a foot long and about 1 inch wide. It starts from the left ventricle, over the heart, from where it divides into several arteries and supplies oxygenated blood to the entire body except the lungs. Aorta has four sections: ascending, arch, descending and abdominal aorta.

74. Pulmonary Artery

The pulmonary artery carries deoxygenated blood from the heart to the lungs. It is one of the only arteries that carry deoxygenated blood. It is relatively short and wide in size and shape. It begins from the bottom of the right ventricle of the heart. And then separates into the right and left pulmonary arteries, which lead to the respective lungs (the right and the left).

75. Pulmonary Vein

The pulmonary vein carries oxygenated blood from the lungs to the left atrium of the heart. It is one of the few veins which carry oxygenated blood. There are four pulmonary veins in the human body, two veins arising from each lung. Each pulmonary vein is linked to a network of capillaries in the alveoli of each lung.

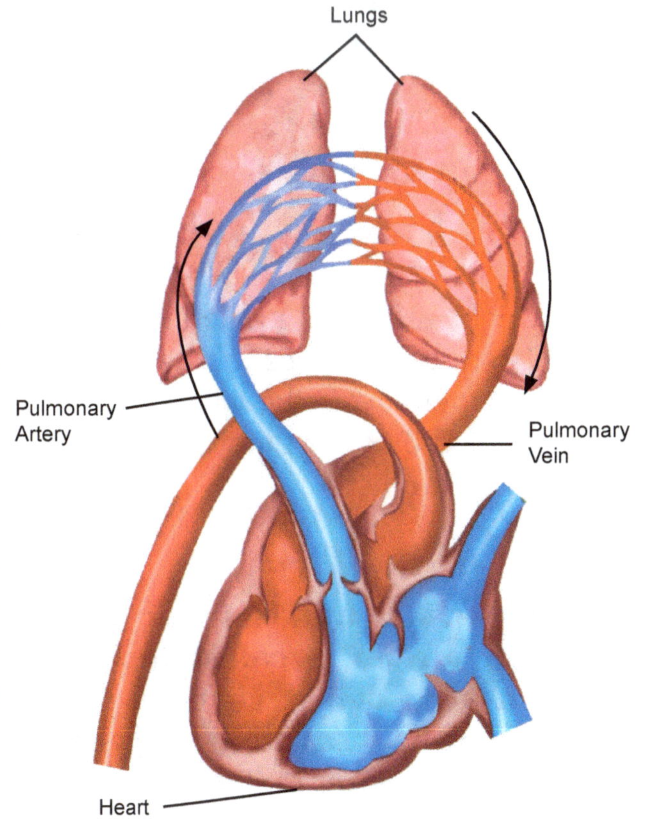

76. Left Ventricle

The human heart has four chambers. Two lower chambers are called ventricles. The left ventricle is connected to the left atrium, on the left side of the heart. It receives blood from the left atrium and pumps it to the aorta. The main function of this ventricle is to pump the oxygenated blood to tissues all over the body. Mitral valve (bicuspid valve) is the medium by which blood passes into the left ventricle, from the left atrium.

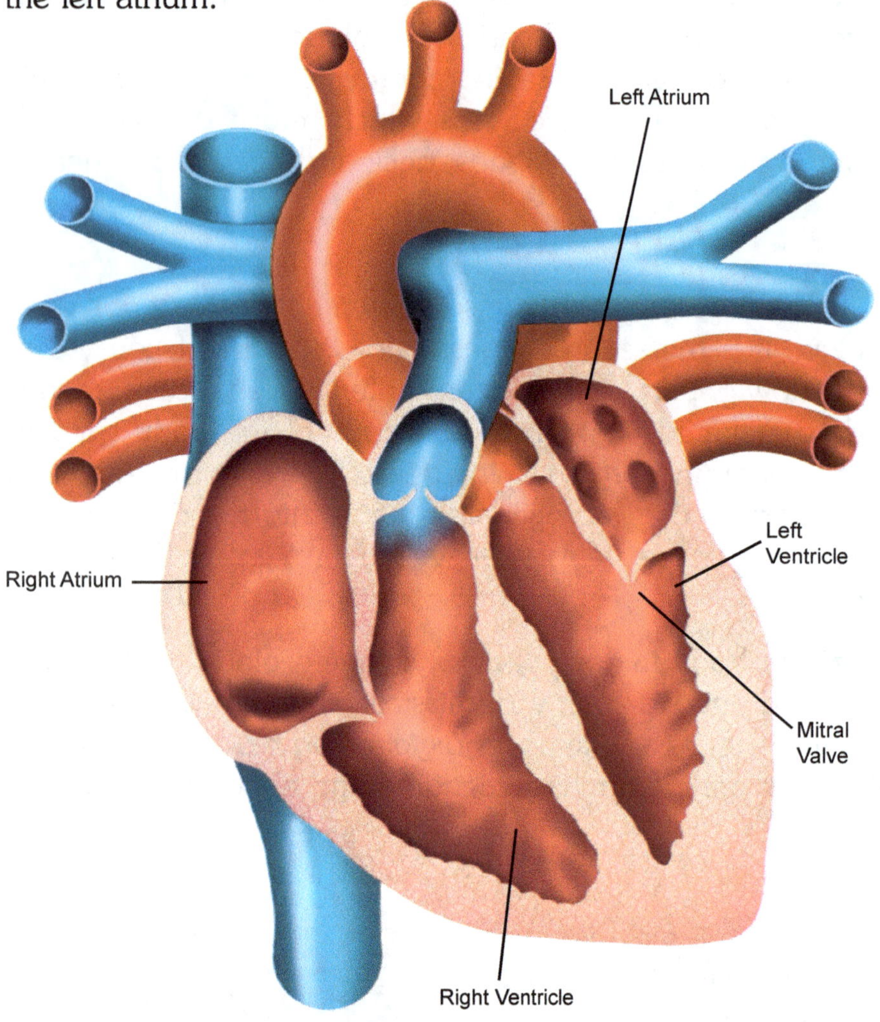

77. Right Ventricle

The right ventricle is located below the right atrium on the right side of the heart. The main function of this ventricle is to pump deoxygenated blood to the lungs. The deoxygenated blood that flows into the right atrium passes through the tricuspid valve and enters the right ventricle. The right ventricle is less muscular as it has to pump the blood to a shorter distance (heart to lung).

78. Left Atrium

The left atrium is the upper-left chamber of the heart. It acts as a vessel for blood returning from the lungs and pumps blood to the left ventricle through the mitral valve. The left atrium holds the oxygen-rich blood that enters from the lungs, through the pulmonary vein.

79. Right Atrium

The right atrium is located on the upper-right side of the heart. It receives deoxygenated blood from the superior and the inferior vena cavae. The deoxygenated blood is pumped to the lungs by the right side of the heart.

A hole in the wall between the right and the left atrium is called the atrial septal defect. This defect changes the sound of the heart-beat as the oxygenated blood gets mixed with the deoxygenated blood and the blood flow gets affected.

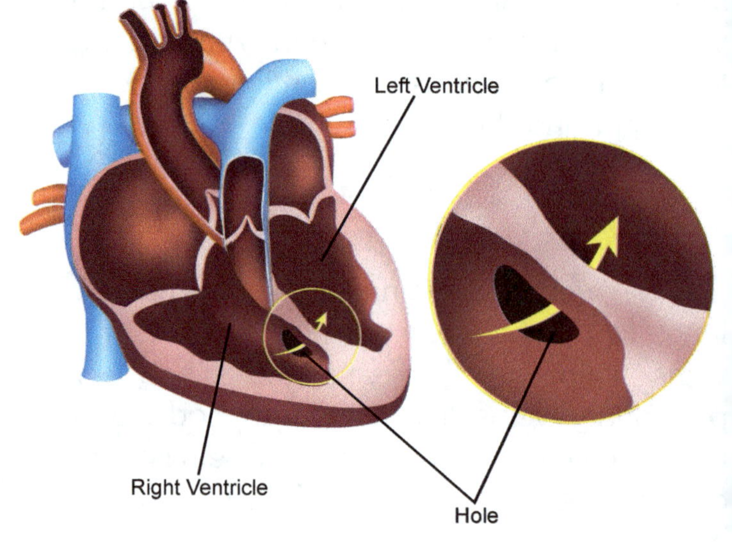

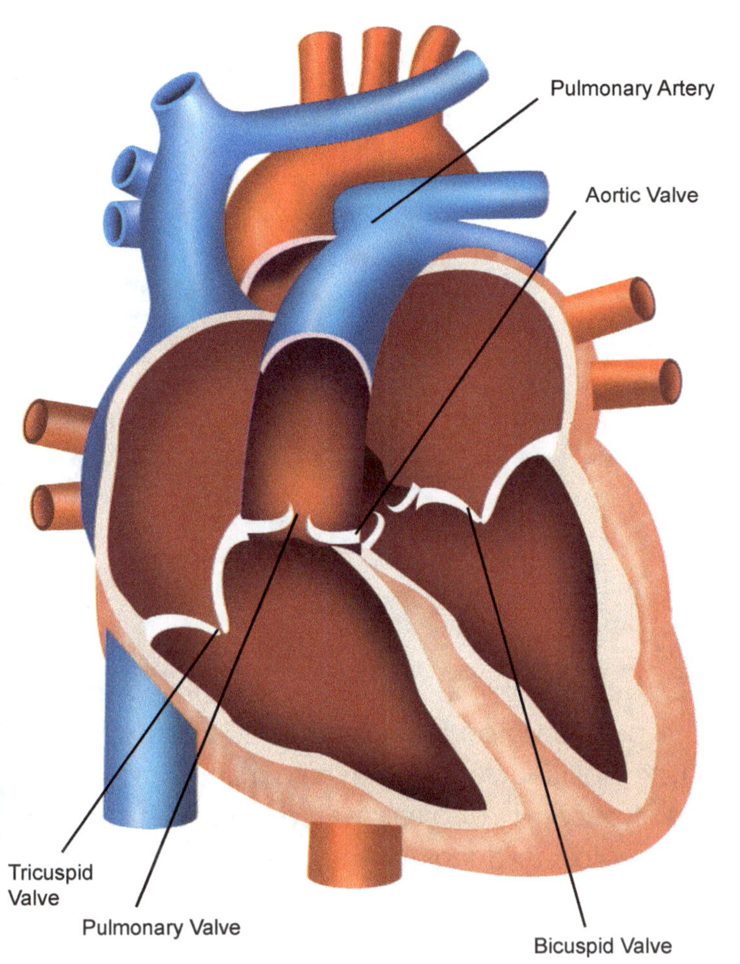

80. Tricuspid and Bicuspid Valve

The tricuspid valve is the valve found between the right atrium and the right ventricle. It basically forms a boundary between the right atrium and the ventricle. It is also called right atrio-ventricular valve. On the other hand, the bicuspid valve is the valve present between the left atrium and the left ventricle. It is also called the mitral valve. They maintain a unidirectional blood flow.

81. Pulmonary and Aortic Valve

The pulmonary valve lies at the edge of the major blood vessel, the pulmonary trunk. Its function is to prevent the backward flow of the blood from the pulmonary artery into the right ventricle. The aortic valve lies between the left ventricle and the aorta. Its function is to prevent the backward flow of the blood from the aorta to the left ventricle. This valve closes when the ventricle relaxes.

82. SA and AV Node

The sino-atrial node (SA node) is located in the right atrium of the heart. The other popular name of the SA node is the sinus node. It is the impulse generating tissue or precisely speaking a natural pacemaker. It generates the sound of the heart beat. The AV node (atrio-ventricular node) is located between the atria and the ventricles of the heart. The AV node generates the impulses from the atria to the ventricles. The AV node is also the natural pacemaker of the heart. The SA node is the primary and the AV node is the secondary pacemaker of the heart.

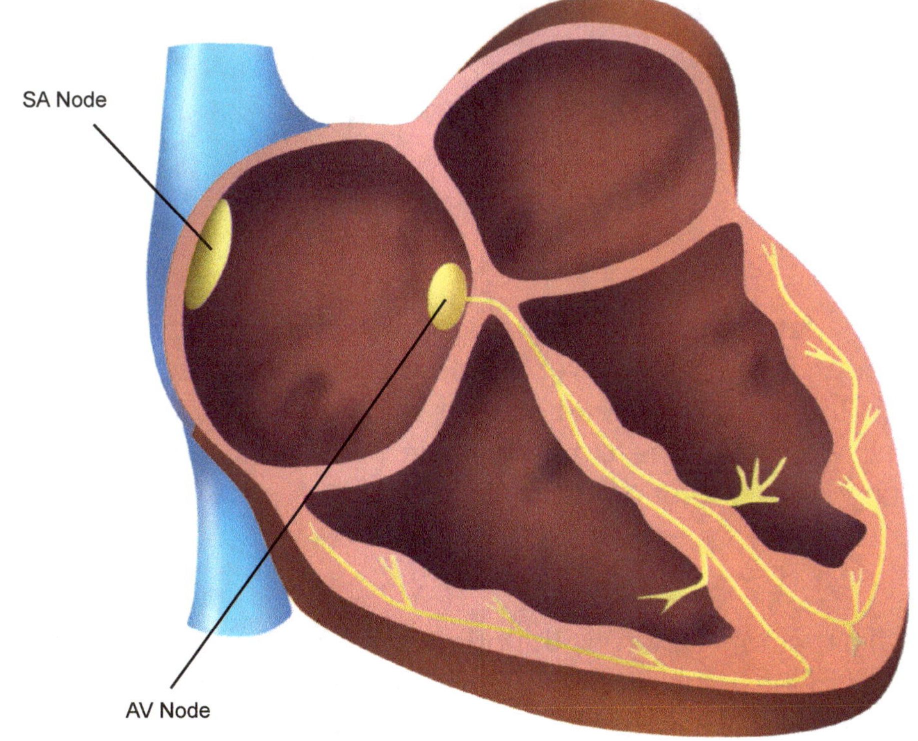

83. Hepatic Artery

The hepatic artery carries blood from the aorta and supplies oxygenated blood to the liver, pancreas and duodenum. The main function of the left and the right hepatic artery is to supply blood (oxygen and nutrients) to the liver.

84. Portal Vein

The portal vein is not a true vein as it does not supply blood directly into the heart. The main function of the hepatic portal vein is to supply metabolic substrates to the liver. The portal venous blood brings the nutrients absorbed by the mucosa of the small intestine to the liver.

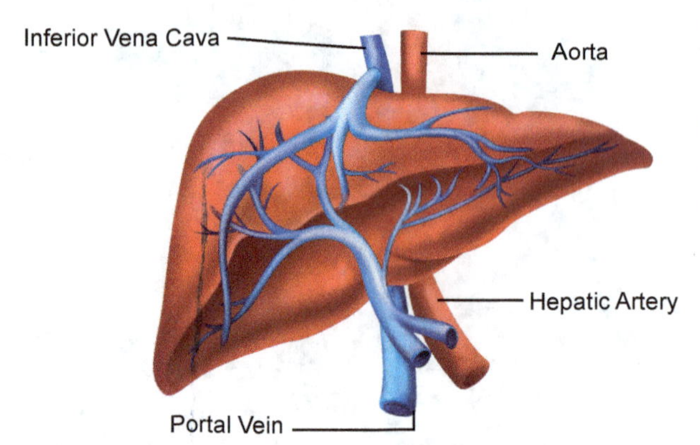

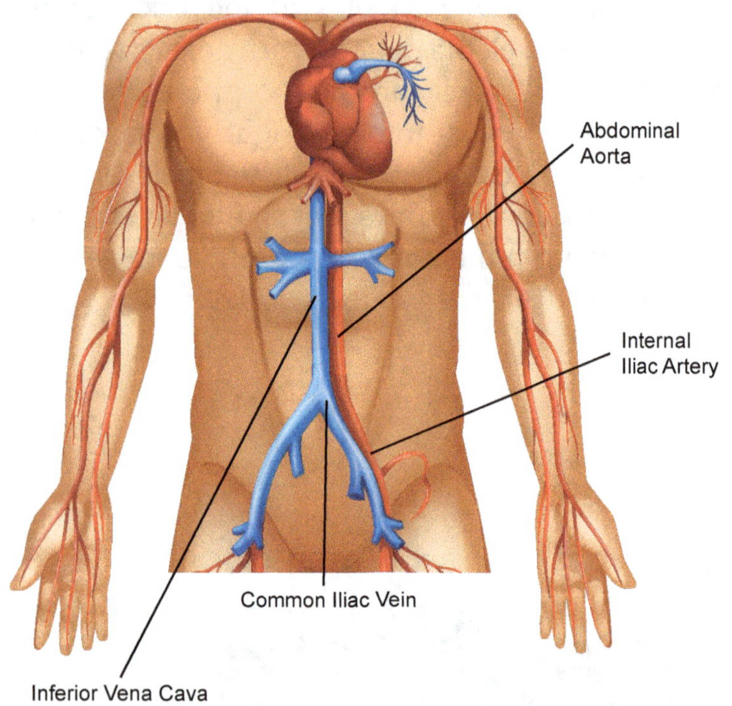

85. Iliac Vein

The common iliac vein is the vein connected to the pelvic region and the leg. It is composed of the internal iliac vein and external iliac vein. These veins transport deoxygenated blood from the pelvic region and legs to the heart via the inferior vena cava.

86. Iliac Artery

The abdominal aorta, a major artery that extends into the abdomen from the aorta, divides into the right and the left common iliac artery. These arteries supply oxygenated blood to the pelvic and the legs (lower limbs).

87. Femoral Vein

The femoral vein is the largest vein in the inner thighs where the leg muscles join the lower abdomen. It returns deoxygenated blood from the leg to the heart via the iliac veins. This vein is part of the femoral triangle. The femoral triangle includes the femoral vein, femoral artery and femoral nerve.

88. Femoral Artery

The femoral artery is the primary artery for providing oxygenated blood to the tissues of the leg, which are found in the lower limb region of the body. These arteries pass through the deep tissues of the leg parallel to the femur.

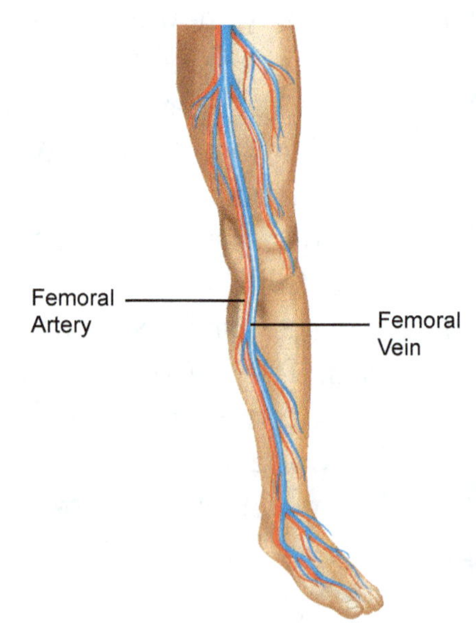

The human heart works like a pump, which beats about 70 times per minute in normal conditions. The heart acts as a dual pump and is comprised of two sets of chambers, two on the right side and two on the left. They are: right and left auricles and right and left ventricles. It is connected with arteries and veins that circulate the blood. These arteries and veins divide to form finer blood vessels called the capillaries.

(1) Circulation starts when the deoxygenated blood (oxygen-poor blood), returning from the body, enters into the right atrium with the help of superior and inferior venae cavae. From here, blood is pumped through the tricuspid valve into the right ventricle.

(2) The deoxygenated blood then travels from the right ventricle into the lungs through the pulmonary artery (through the pulmonary semi-lunar valve).

(3) In the lungs, the blood gets oxygenated and then the oxygenated (oxygen-rich) blood returns to the left atrium from the lungs through the pulmonary veins.

(4) The left atrium contracts and pumps the blood to the left ventricle with the help of the bicuspid (mitral) valve. Finally, the oxygenated blood is pumped by the left ventricle out through the aorta and then to the entire body.

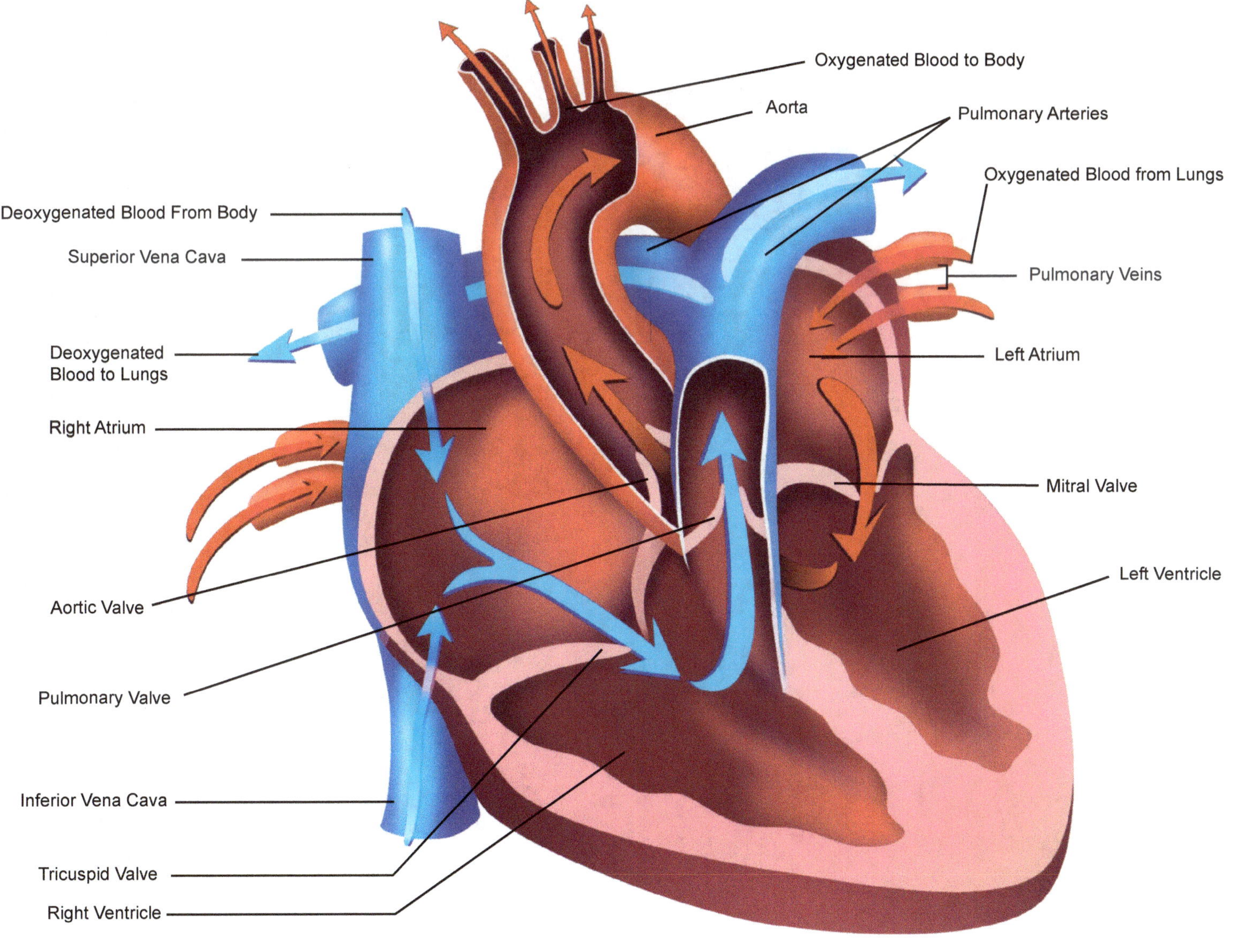

Blockage of coronary arteries is also called CAD or coronary heart disease. It is the most common cause of illness and death. This disease is a group of problems that occur when the heart and blood vessels are not working the way they should.

The disease occurs when our arteries become narrowed due to gradual build-up of fatty material within their walls. The initial stage is indicated by the occurrence of angina. Angina or chest pain occurs when the heart does not have enough oxygen; this in extreme stages leads to a heart attack. During a heart attack, the heart does not get any oxygen at all. During a heart attack, some of the heart muscles can die due to the lack of oxygen. The major causes of CAD are lifestyle issues (sedentary lifestyle) and bad food habits. This problem can be averted by having a healthy lifestyle. A healthy lifestyle can decrease the risk of CAD. For example: being physically active, eating a healthy diet that is low in fat, achieving and maintaining a healthy weight, limiting alcohol use, etc.

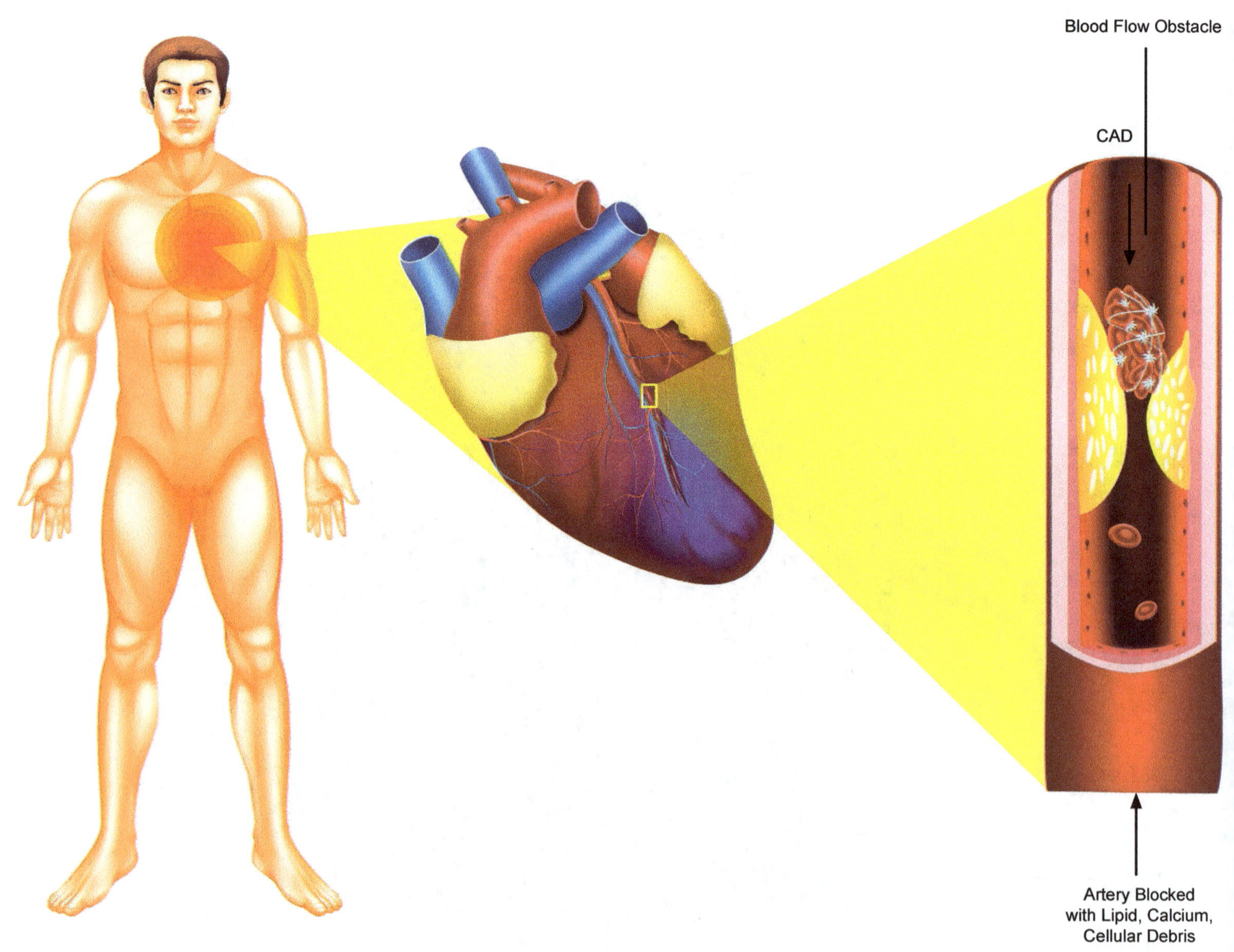

89. Lymphatic System

The lymphatic system is simply referred as the drainage system of the body. It collects the excess fluid from the tissues in the body and returns it to the blood system or the central circulatory system. The lymphatic system is well equipped with vessels. It supports the immune system. The major parts of this system are: lymphatic capillaries and lymph nodes, tonsils, thymus gland and spleen. This system carries bacteria and dead blood cells that are to be destroyed, to the lymph nodes and the spleen. This network collects the water within the blood plasma, which gets forced out during the passage of the blood through the capillaries.

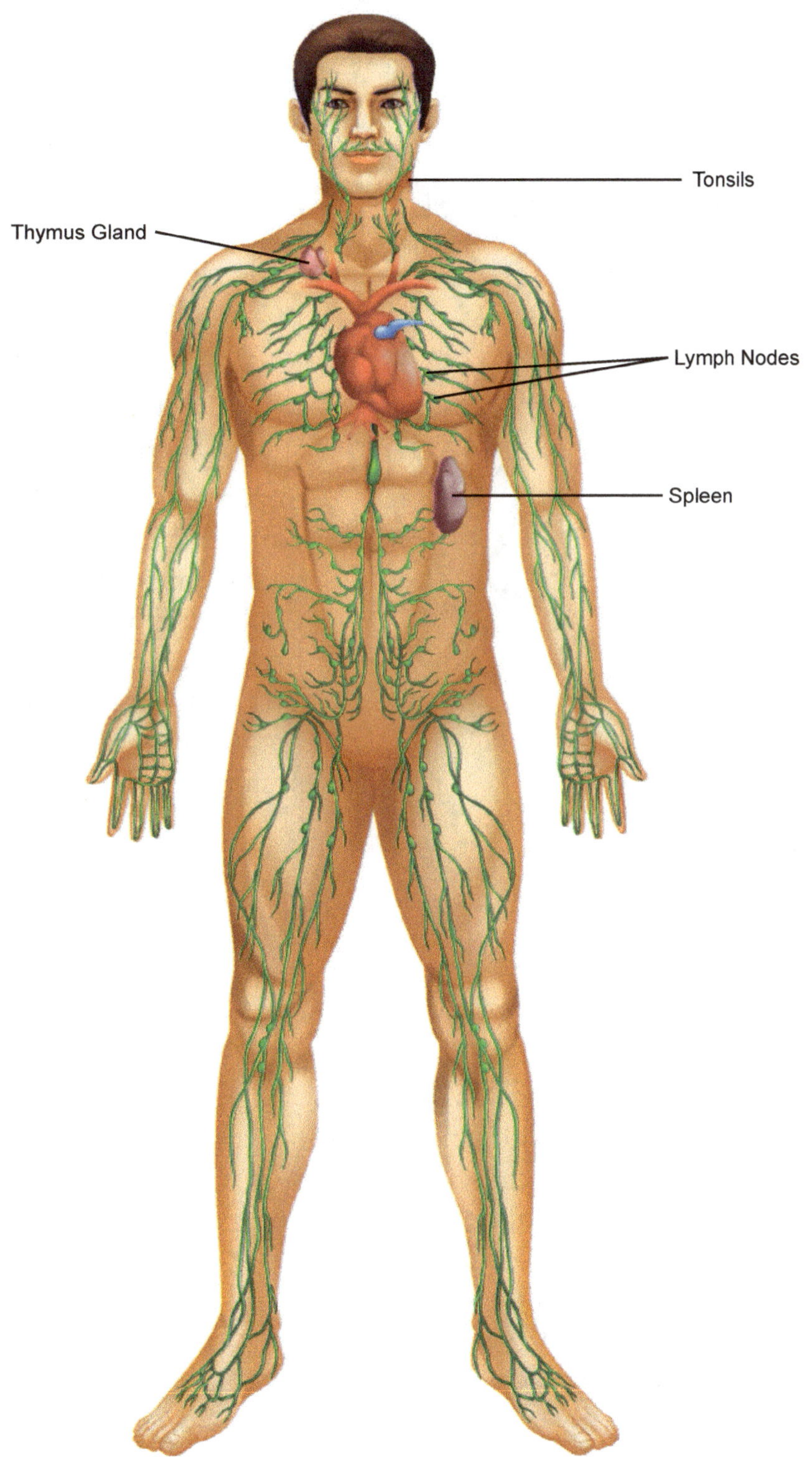

90. Tonsils

Tonsils are the part of the immune system of the body. They constitute the first line of defence of the body. Tonsils are located at the top of the pharynx, on each side of the back of the throat. There are three pairs of tonsils: the pharyngeal, the palatine tonsils, and the lingual tonsils. The main function of the tonsils is to protect against harmful substances that may enter the body through the nose and the mouth.

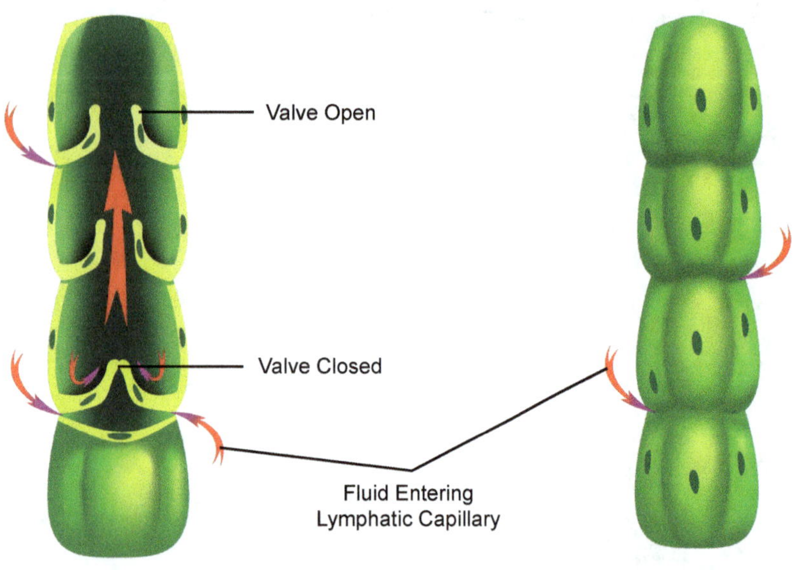

Lymph

A colourless fluid that is rich in white blood cells

91. Lymph Vessels

Lymph vessels are similar in structure to the veins but they bear several valves on its surface. These valves impart a beaded appearance to the lymph vessels. They move corresponding to veins and arteries. The valves present on the lymph vessels prevent the back flow of the lymph, once the lymph has entered the main circulatory system. The muscles of the lymph vessel walls contract to help move lymph through the system.

92. Lymph Node

A lymph node is like a filter ball through which lymph passes through before entering the heart. The lymph node walls are perforated tissues which give these nodes a spongy appearance. These filters remove bacteria and help with the immune response; they are essential to the functioning of the immune system. The main group lies in the neck, armpit, chest and abdomen. When a body has an infection in it, these lymph nodes swell to enhance the filtration capacity.

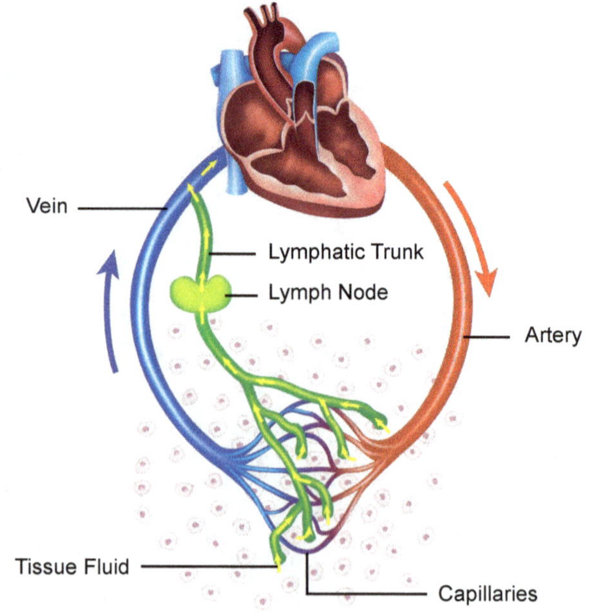

93. Lymphatic (Lymph) Duct

A lymph duct collects lymph from various tissues and then moves it to the blood vessels. There are two lymph ducts in the body: thoracic (left lymphatic duct) and right lymphatic duct. The thoracic duct moves along the abdomen to the neck. It collects lymph from the digestive tract. The right lymphatic duct (a smaller vessel) collects lymph from the right upper limb, right side of thorax and right halves of the head and the neck.

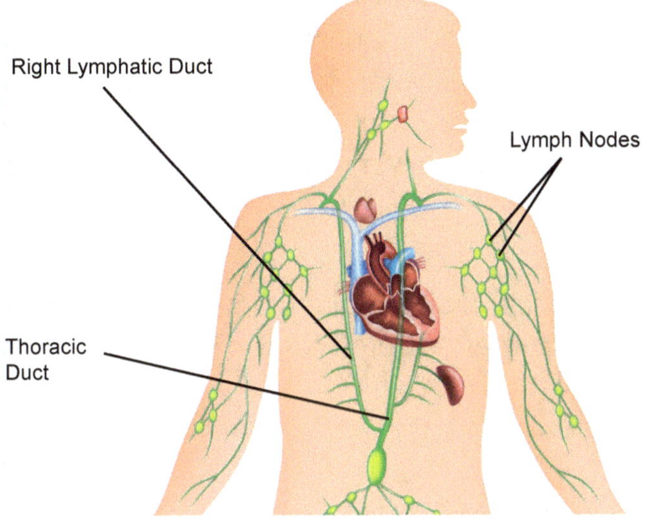

94. Bone Marrow

The bone marrow is a red or yellow soft, spongy, fatty tissue present inside the bones. It is also called the myeloid tissue. The extent to which the red blood cells are present in the bone marrow decides the colour of the marrow. If the marrow has prevalent fat tissues then it appears yellow in colour. The lymphocytes are produced in the marrow, but they reach their mature form in the lymphoid organs.

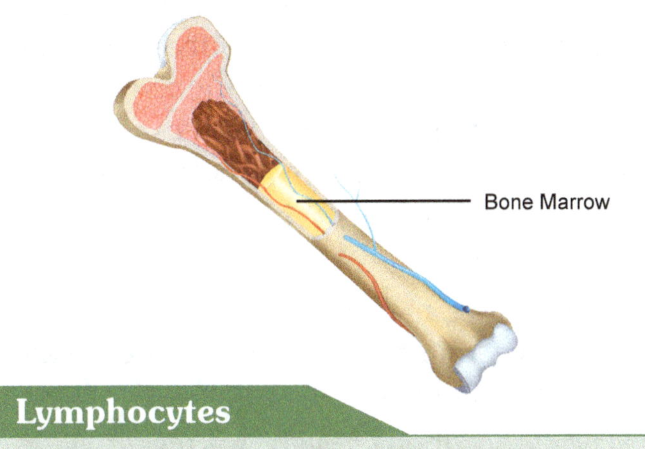

Lymphocytes

They are a form of white blood cells that are small in size.

95. Spleen

Spleen is the largest organ of adult lymphatic system, located behind the stomach, in the abdominal cavity. It resembles a lymph node, but it is larger than lymph nodes. It is made up of two types of tissues. (1) Red pulp that removes bacteria and lymphocytes (white blood cells) and macrophages. (2) White pulp is mainly lymphocytes. Spleen filters the blood and brings blood into contact with lymphocytes, which destroy harmful substances.

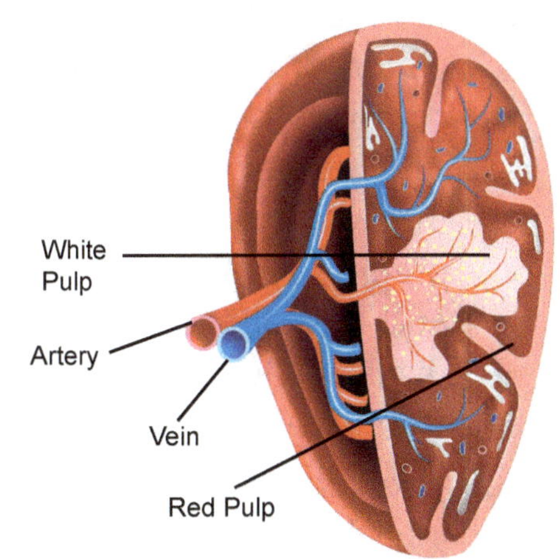

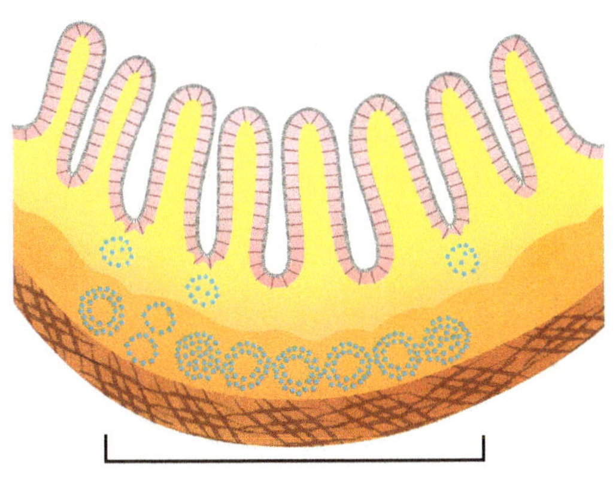

96. Peyer's Patch

Peyer's patch is a set of round or oval nodules, mostly found in the lowest portion (ileum) of the small intestine. These nodules of lymphatic cells aggregate and form bundles or patches. These nodules exercise protective function in the intestine. They protect the intestine from bacterial invasion. During the typhoid fever, these are the site of inflammation.

97. Digestive System

Food is needed for growth. It acts as a fuel for the production of heat and energy. The digestive system receives the food and breaks it down into simpler components so that it may be used in the body. The entire process of the reception of food and its breaking down into simpler components is called digestion. The human digestive system consists of alimentary canal and its glands. The major parts of the digestive system are: mouth, oesophagus (food pipe), stomach, small intestine, large intestine, rectum, liver and pancreas. The human alimentary canal is basically about 9 metres long tube that runs from the mouth to the anus.

Digestion of Food

The food that we eat is composed of complex components. These components are needed to be broken down into simpler form so that they may be used in the body. The entire process of breaking down the complex nutrients into simpler form is called digestion. The process of digestion starts from the mouth and ends in the small intestine. When the food is converted into simpler form, it can be absorbed into the bloodstream. Once nutrients are taken up by the bloodstream, they can be distributed to and used by the body cells.

The digestion process:

a. Food enters the body through the mouth where it is mechanically broken down into smaller form. The masticated form of food is called bolus. The enzymes secreted by the salivary glands start the process of digestion.

b. The food then travels to the pharynx and the oesophagus. From the oesophagus, food enters the stomach.

c. In the stomach, the food is churned and the digestion of complex nutrients takes place. The stomach is filled with acid that activates the enzymes, breaks down the food further and kills the germs. The semi-digested food that leaves the stomach is referred as chyme.

d. The chyme enters the small intestine where it is digested completely and the nutrients are absorbed.

e. The food devoid of nutrients then enters the large intestine where excess water is absorbed and the semi-solid residue is expelled out of the body through the rectum.

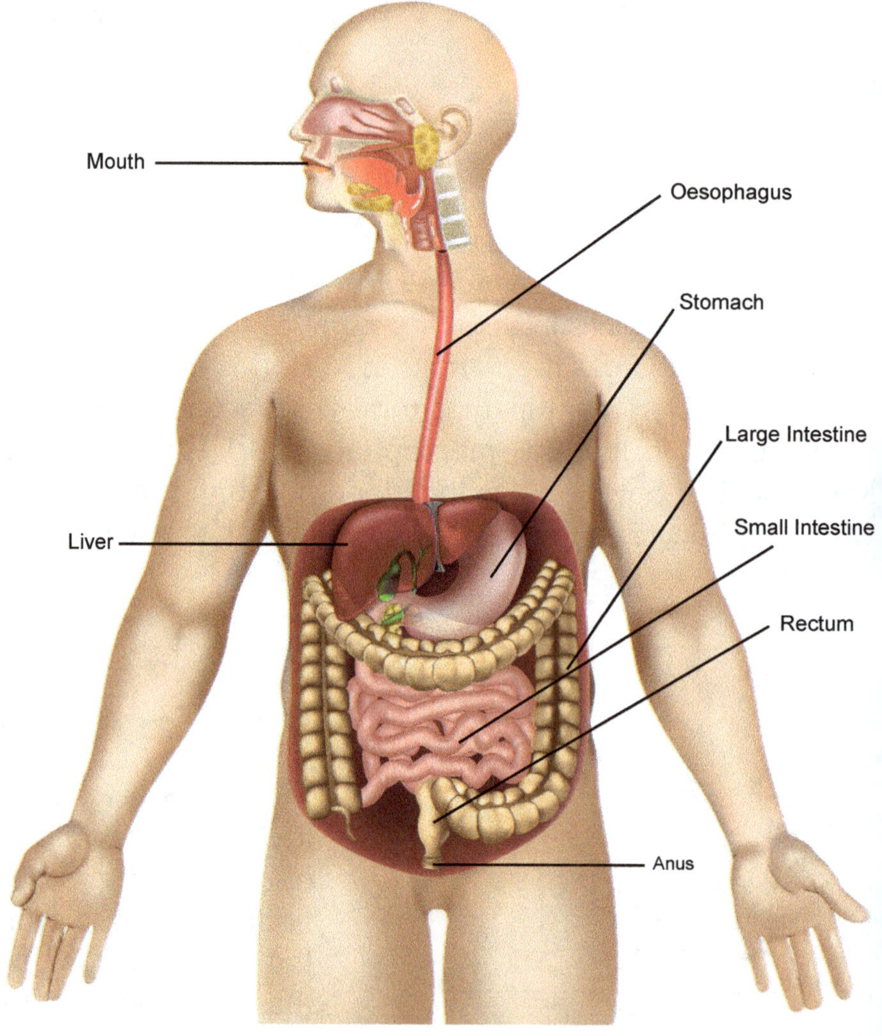

98. Mouth

Food begins its journey from the mouth. The main parts of the mouth are: teeth, tongue and salivary glands. In the mouth, food particles are broken down physically with the help of teeth. It is known as mechanical digestion. Saliva, the watery secretion of the salivary glands, moistens and lubricates the food. Saliva starts the chemical digestion of the food by breaking down the starch present in the food.

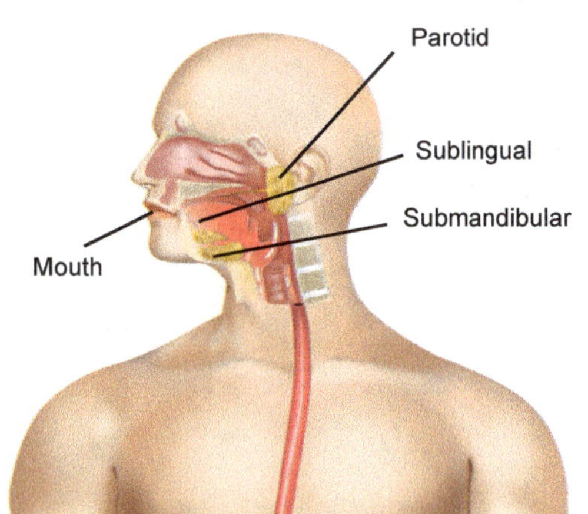

99. Salivary Glands

As food is chewed, it is mixed with the saliva secreted from the salivary glands. Salivary glands are a group of sac-like alveoli, which form small lobules. These lobules house small ducts which secrete saliva. The principle salivary glands are: parotid, submandibular and sublingual. The saliva moistens the food and starts the chemical digestion of food by secreting starch-digesting enzyme amylase (ptylin). Starch is broken down into soluble form of sugar and maltose.

Lobules

Tiny lobe-type structures

100. Teeth

Teeth play an important role in the digestive process. The mouth contains teeth which masticate the food. Mastication means biting and grinding of food into smaller pieces between the upper and the lower teeth. This allows the enzymes (present in saliva) to mix well with food and hence swallowed more easily. If the food is not chewed properly, the digestion process becomes ineffective.

101. Palate

The palate is the roof of the mouth, divided into two parts: hard palate at the front, and soft palate at the back. The hard palate is supported by the bones of the skull. The soft palate is made up of skeletal muscles and connective tissues. The main function of the palate is to prevent food from entering the nasal cavity during swallowing.

102. Uvula

The uvula is a soft and fleshy small hanging lobe, which is an extended part of the soft palate. It stretches out in the back of the throat. It is composed of soft connective tissues surrounded by an epithelial layer. It has two major roles: (1) it blocks the internal opening of the nose at the time of swallowing the food. It also protects the food from entering the wind pipe. (2) it also plays an important role in producing proper speech.

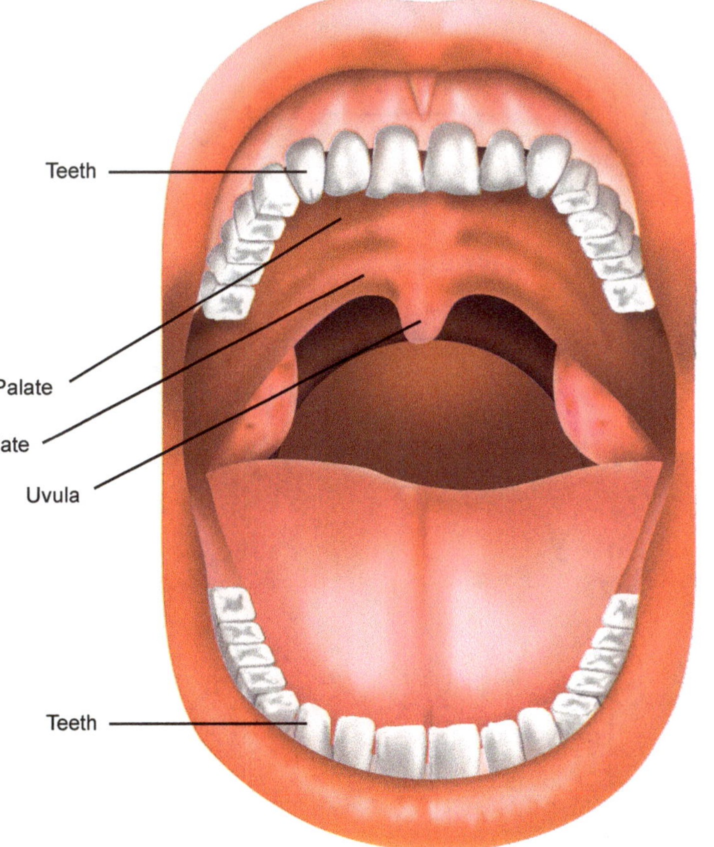

103. Pharynx Chamber

The pharynx is a cone-shaped passageway that lies behind the nose, mouth and larynx. The pharynx chamber plays both respiratory and digestive functions. The pharynx chamber consists of the naso pharynx, oral pharynx and laryngeal pharynx. The chief muscles of the pharynx are constrictor muscles which contract, when food is received into the pharynx, and force it to the oesophagus.

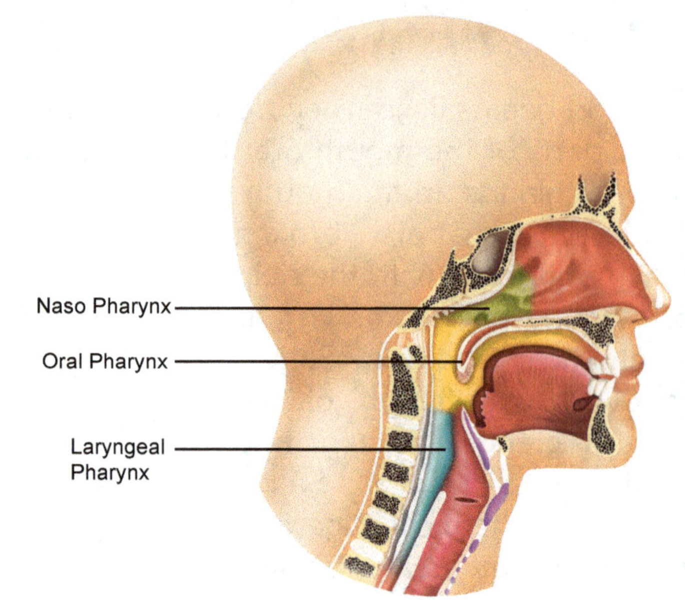

104. Oesophagus

The oesophagus is a hollow muscular tube, also known as the food pipe or gullet. It is a connecting tube between the mouth and the stomach. It is located behind the trachea. The oesophagus consists of four coats of tissues. The movement of the tissue layers is responsible to move the food towards the stomach from the pharynx.

Peristalsis

The contraction of muscles in order to move something, in case of oesophagus. It is the movement of food towards the stomach.

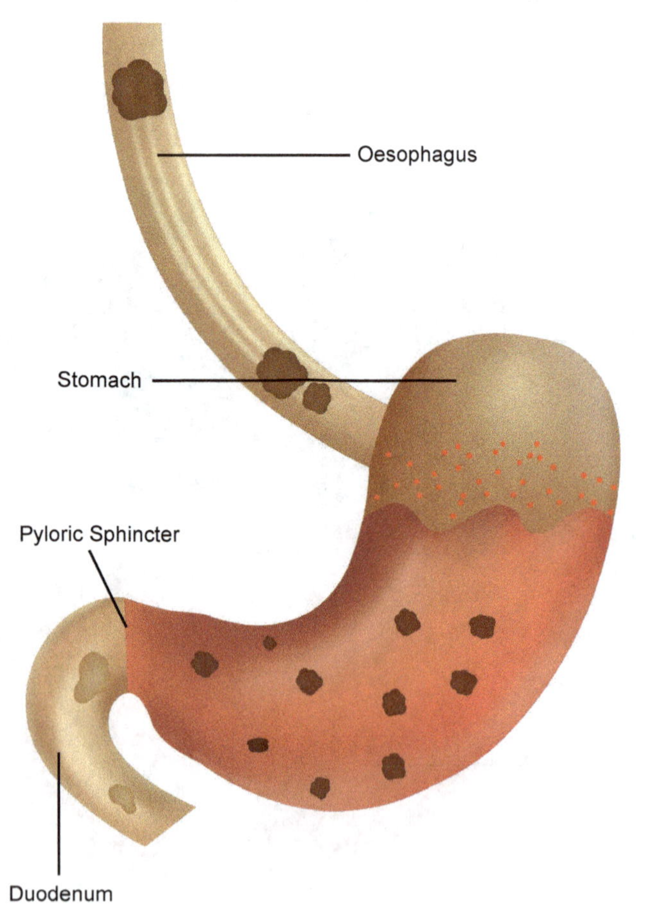

105. Stomach

The stomach is the main part of the digestive system. It is also called food storage-tank of the body. It is a muscular, hollow organ that is open at both the ends. It lies between the oesophagus and the duodenum (the first part of the small intestine). While storing the food temporarily, muscular contractions of the stomach mix the food with the digestive juices. The digestive juices contain several enzymes that digest the food.

106. Pyloric Sphincter

The pyloric sphincter is a narrow, thick ring of smooth muscle located at the bottom of the stomach. The two important functions performed by the pyloric sphincter are: (1) it controls the movement of the stomach contents from the stomach into the duodenum and (2) it maintains healthy functioning of the digestive tract. The pyloric sphincter is actually a valve that regulates digestion.

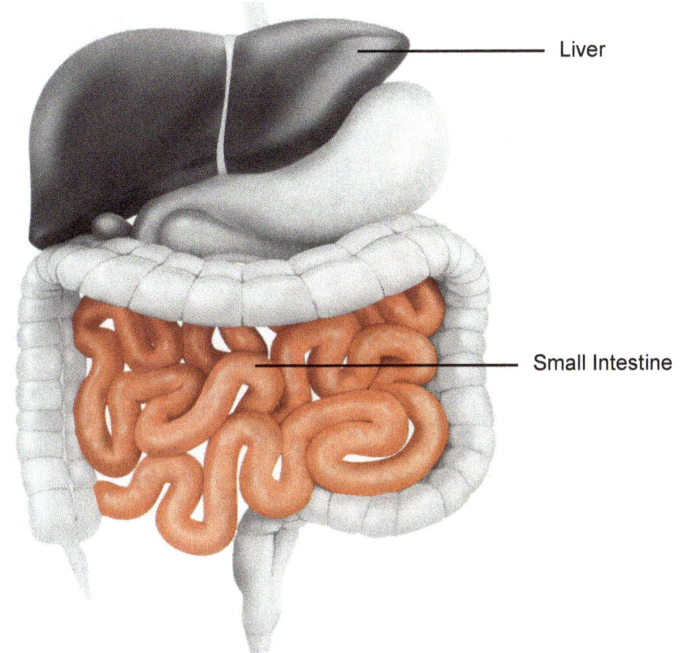

107. Small Intestine

The small intestine completes the process of digestion. The food before reaching the duodenum undergoes acid treatment and chemical digestion. The form of food that reaches the duodenum is called the chyme. Here, the digestion and absorption process of the nutrients in the chyme gets completed. Pancreatic and intestinal enzymes play an important role in the digestion of food in the intestine.

108. Duodenum

The duodenum is the upper (first) part of the small intestine. Its length ranges from about 23 to 28 cm. It resembles a horse shoe in shape. The bile and the pancreatic ducts open in the duodenum. It is divided into four segments: the superior, descending, horizontal and ascending duodenum. The food spends a lot of time in the duodenum as maximum digestion and absorption takes place in this part of the small intestine.

109. Jejunum

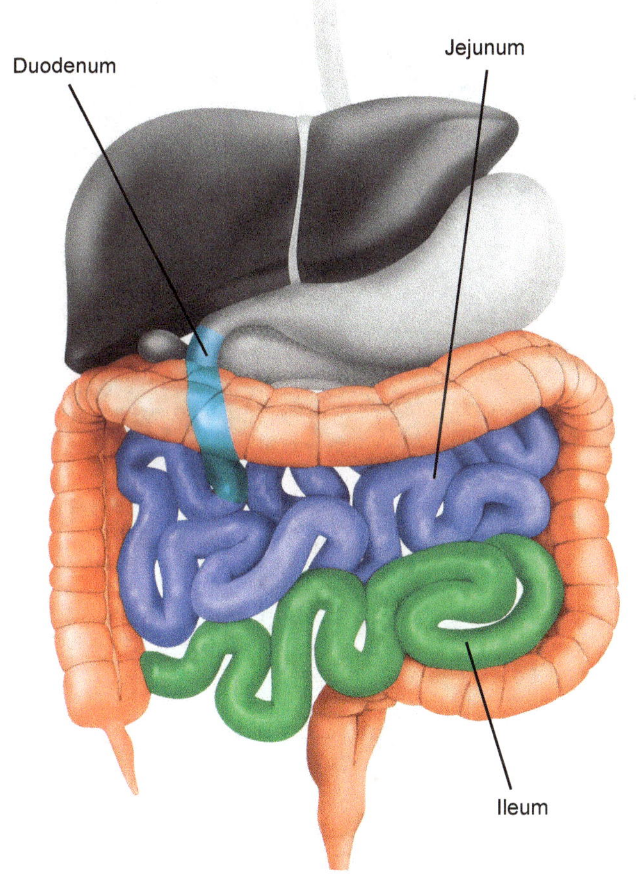

The second part of the small intestine is the jejunum. The chyme moves to the jejunum, after being digested and partly absorbed in the duodenum. The inside walls in the jejunum absorb the nutrients in the chyme. The presence of the number of villi increases the surface area of the jejunum manifold which, in turn, absorbs nutrients present in the chyme. The muscular movement of the jejunum is rapid and vigourous to facilitate absorption.

110. Ileum

The ileum is the last and longest part of the small intestine, located in the lower abdomen. The muscular movements in this part of intestine are slow. Structurally, this part is narrower and thinner than the previous two parts of the small intestine. It absorbs bile acids and vitamin B_{12}. Bile acids are then returned to the liver for the formation of bile, and vitamin B_{12} is used by the body for making nerve cells and red blood cells.

111. Villus

The absorption of the digested food takes place entirely in the small intestine through two channels, the capillary blood vessels and the lymphatics of the villi. A villus looks like a small, finger that lies above the intestinal wall surface. Villi are found in a large number in the beginning of the small intestine. But towards the end of the tract, they reduce in number. The lacteals in the villi absorb the fats, while all the other nutrients directly pass into the capillary blood vessels of the villi.

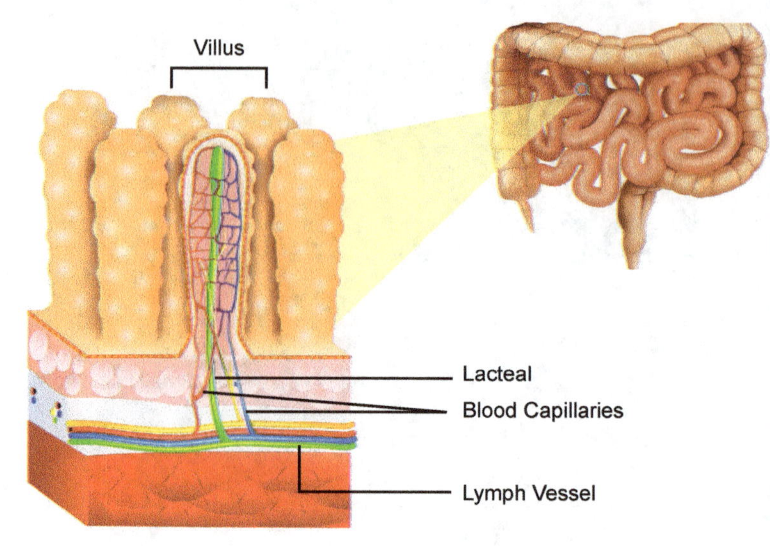

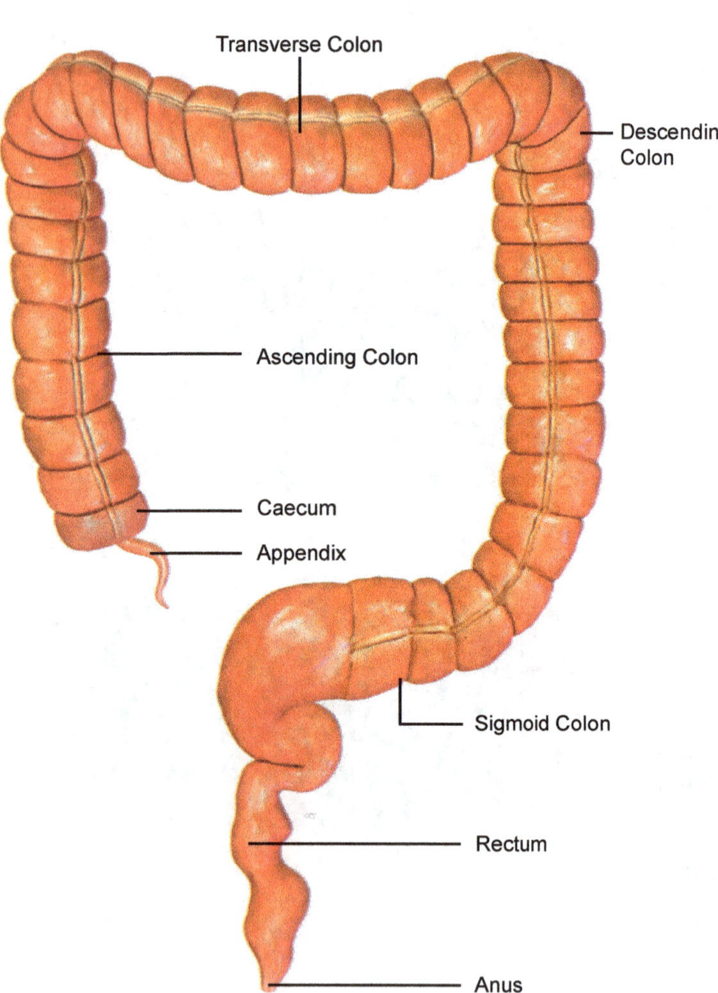

112. Large Intestine

The large intestine is also known as colon. It is a long continuous tube-like tract through which food residue passes before defecation. The colon begins as a dilated pouch, the caecum, to which appendix is attached. The large intestine does not take part in the digestion or the absorption of the food. The content that reaches the large intestine is devoid of nutrients. The large intestinal walls absorb the water in the residue and the soft-solid is passed towards the rectum. Peristalsis is very slow in the colon.

113. Rectum

The rectum is the last portion of the large intestine. It is normally empty until just before defecation. In a person of regular habit the call to defecate occurs at about the same time each day. During defecation strong peristalsis occurs in the colon. The rectum acts as a temporary storage site for faeces, which expels solid waste through the anus.

114. Appendix

The appendix is also known as the vermix. It is a pouch-like structure of tissues, located in the lower abdominal at the right-hand side. It resembles a worm. It is a narrow tube about four inches long. Its function is not known completely, but according to a few theories, it acts as a storehouse for storing good bacteria of the stomach.

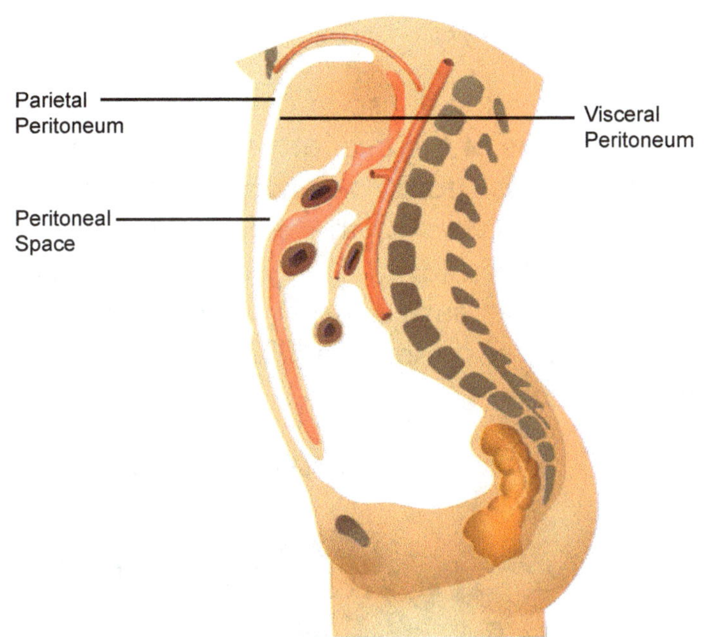

115. Peritoneum

The peritoneum is a dual layered membrane. One is the parietal peritoneum that covers the abdominal wall and the other is the visceral peritoneum that covers the abdominal organs. The space between these two layers is called the peritoneal space. The layer creates a smooth lining over the organs and helps them to slide upon one another smoothly. It attaches the organs with one another and keeps them in a definite position.

116. Liver

The liver is the largest gland in the body, divided into two main lobes, the right and the left. It secretes bile into the small intestine. It is the largest chemical factory that carries out most of the intermediate metabolic functions. For example: (1) it breaks down and builds up new biological molecules, stores vitamins and ions, destroys old blood cells and other poisonous material (toxins); (2) it helps in the formation of urea, and prepares the fat for final breakdown; and (3) it plays an important role in the body's immunity and temperature regulation.

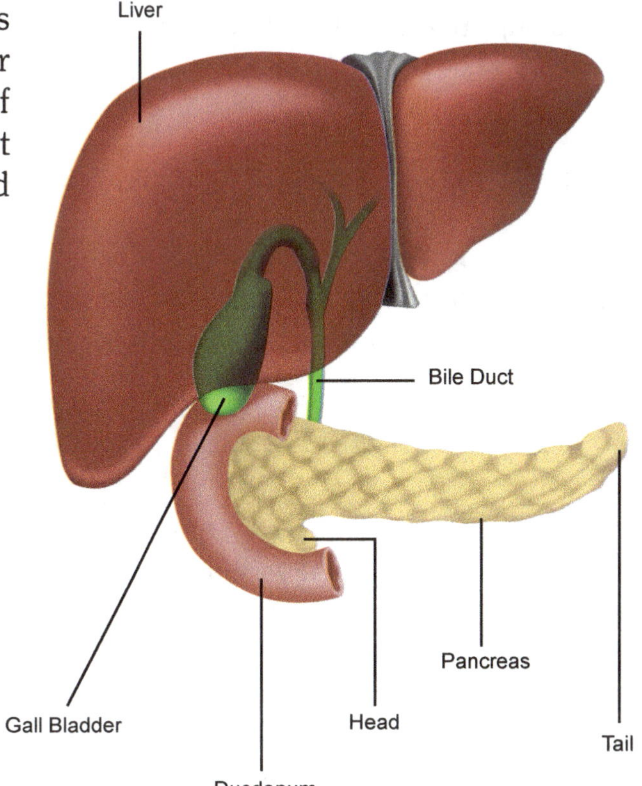

117. Gall Bladder

The gall bladder looks like a pear fruit. It lies under the liver, on the right side of the abdomen. The gall bladder stores the bile produced by the liver and concentrates it further. The stored bile is released into the duodenum by the contraction of the gall bladder, half an hour after the consumption of food. It is an important part of the body, crucial for the digestion of fat, as it stores bile.

118. Pancreas

The pancreas is a compound gland, very similar to the salivary gland. It extends from the duodenum to the spleen. The pancreas has three parts, the head, the body and the tail. It is a dual organ. (1) it forms pancreatic juices that contain enzymes and electrolytes. When chyme enters the duodenum, pancreatic juice is released into the duodenum by the pancreas. (2) it acts as an endocrine organ, as it manages the secretion of insulin and glucagon (important hormone for sugar level regulation) in the body.

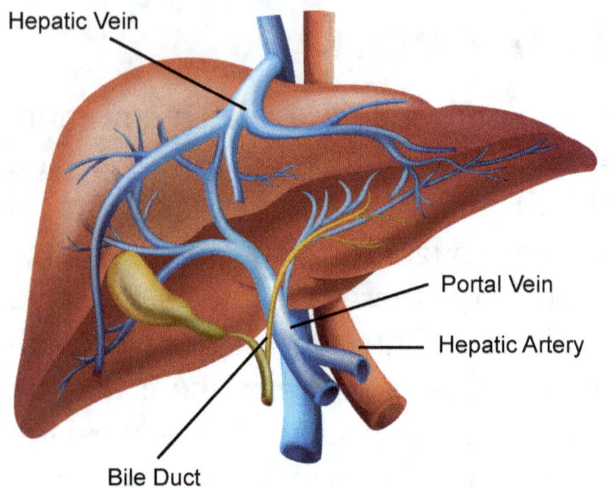

119. Liver Vessels

The liver vessels help in the transport of substances to and from the liver. Four vessels of the liver are as follows: (1) the hepatic artery that arises from the aorta and supplies oxygenated blood to the liver; (2) the portal vein supplies oxygenated blood to the liver; (3) the hepatic vein returns the blood from the liver to the heart; and (4) the bile ducts that are formed by the union of the bile capillaries which collect the bile from the liver cells.

120. Bile

The bile is a liquid secreted by the liver. It plays an important role in the digestion of food. The bile is composed of bile pigments, bile salts, cholesterol and phospholipids. The bile helps break down fats and in the activation of enzymes required for the digestion of fat. The human body secretes approximately 1 litre of bile every day.

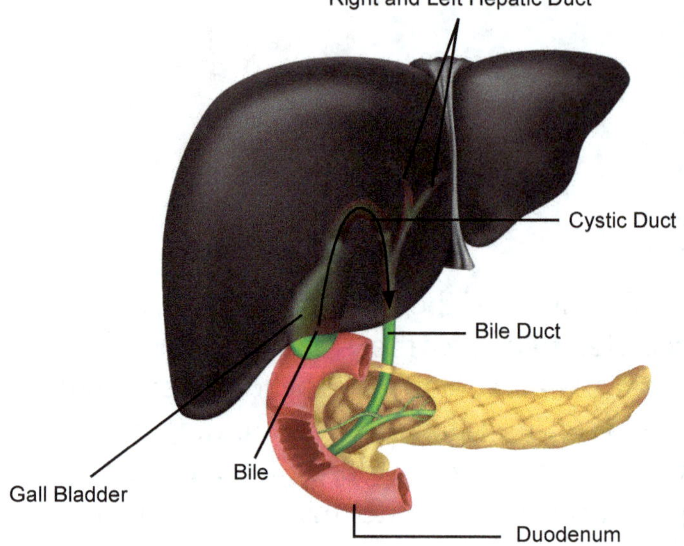

121. Digestive Enzymes

Food is composed of carbohydrates, proteins, fats, vitamins, minerals and water. The digestive enzymes secreted by the digestive system helps break down the complex nutrients into simpler form. The various enzymes secreted by the human body are:

Major Digestive Enzymes

Enzyme	Produced In
Carbohydrate Digestion :	
Salivary amylase	Salivary glands
Pancreatic amylase	Pancreas
Maltase	Small intestine
Protein Digestion :	
Pepsin	Gastric glands
Trypsin	Pancreas
Peptidases	Small intestine
Nucleic Acid Digestion :	
Nuclease	Pancreas
Nucleosidases	Pancreas
Fat Digestion :	
Lipase	Pancreas

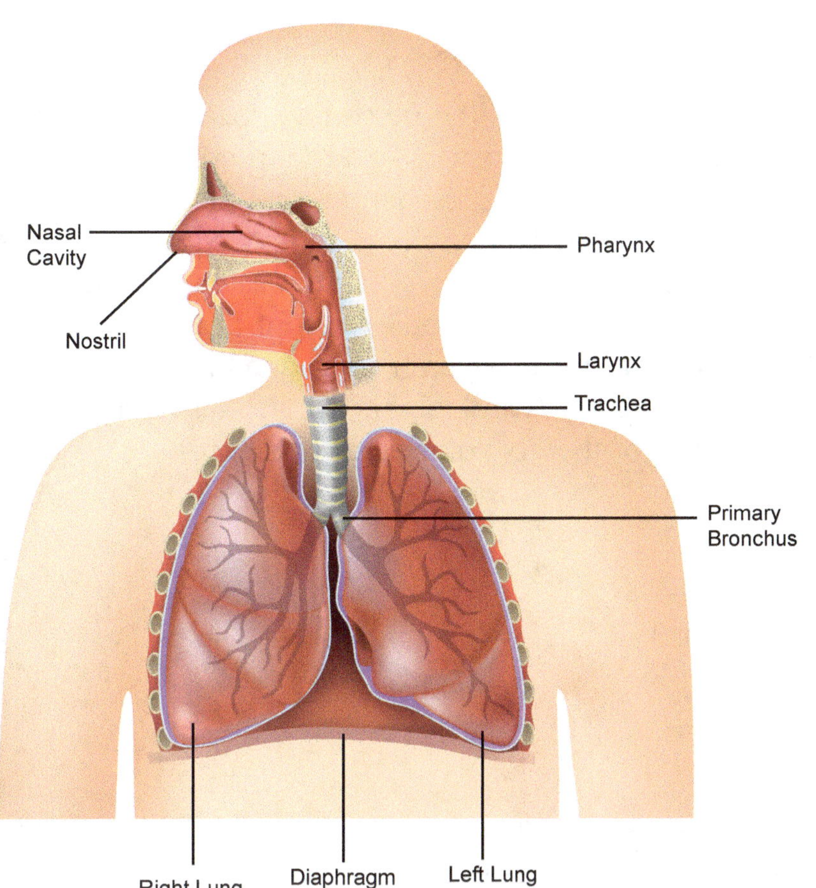

122. Respiratory System

The respiratory system is a set of organs that help a human being to breathe. Breathing is the process of inhaling oxygen and exhaling carbon dioxide. The respiratory passage consists of the nose, nasal cavity, pharynx, trachea, bronchi, lungs and diaphragm. Human beings can involuntarily control the process of breathing but overall the process is controlled and coordinated through the nervous system.

123. Nostril

The nose is made of flesh covered bone and cartilage (dense connective tissue). The first part of the respiratory system through which air is inhaled into the body is the nostrils (openings at the front of the nose). The two nostrils are separated by the septum. The inner lining of the nostril is covered with a thin layer of skin which is covered with coarse hair. The hair acts as a protective covering for the nose, as it prevents the inhalation of dust particles.

124. Nasal Cavity

The nostrils open into the nasal cavity which is the space inside the nose between the base of the skull and the roof of the mouth. It connects the nostrils to the upper part of the pharynx (throat). The whole cavity is covered with mucous membrane (lining that secretes slimy fluid) and tiny hair called cilia. The nasal cavity also contains the olfactory apparatus or epithelium that supports the sense of smell. The air that passes through the cavity is filtered through the cilia.

125. Sinuses

The respiratory sinuses are air-filled, mucous-membrane lined cavities within the skull and facial bones surrounding the nose. There are four pairs of sinuses in the body that produce mucous. This mucous is drained out through the nasal cavity. Sinuses help to warm and moisten the inhaled air. They produce mucus that helps to trap dust, microbes and other particles. Sinus cavities help in speech production, too.

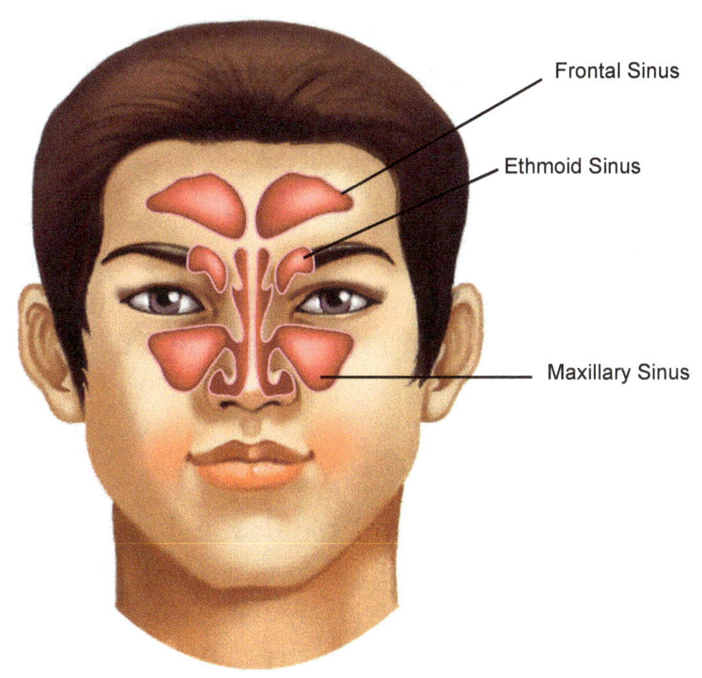

126. Pharynx

The pharynx is a muscular tube which extends from the base of the skull to the oesophagus. It makes a bridge between the nasal cavity and the larynx and the oesophagus. It is common to both the respiratory tract and the digestive tract. In the respiratory tract it acts as an air passage during breathing, and in the digestive tract it acts as a food passage during swallowing.

127. Larynx

The larynx is the voice box, located above the trachea. This organ of vocal sound production also serves as an air passage between the pharynx and the trachea. The larynx is composed of the pieces of cartilage. The largest of these is thyroid cartilage and then Adam's apple in front of the neck. The larynx forms an opening between the pharynx and the trachea (wind pipe). Larynx also provides a base for the epiglottis and vocal cords.

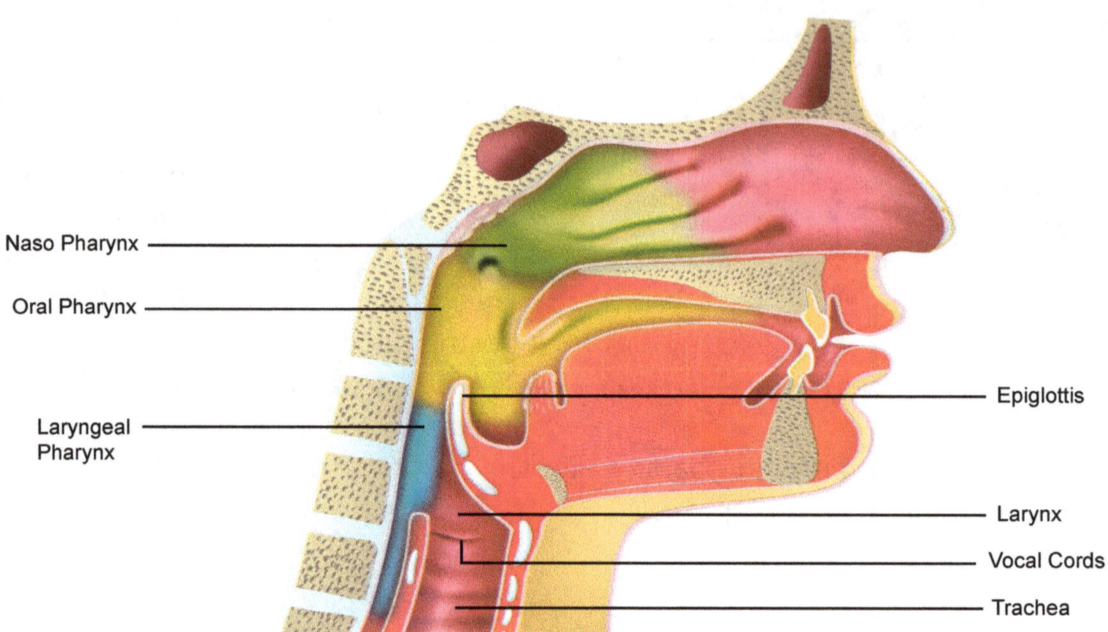

128. Epiglottis

Epiglottis is a flexible flap made up of cartilaginous tissues, located behind the tongue. It helps to close off the larynx during the swallowing of food. This is a very crucial function. This situation can make a human being very uncomfortable. So, it performs an important function by guiding food towards the oesophagus.

129. Vocal Cords

Vocal cords are two belts of tissue stretched across the larynx. The voice is produced due to the vibration of the cords. These cords vibrate due to the air passing through the glottis. Various muscles attached to the larynx control the production of the voice. Other organs of sound production and speech include the mouth, tongue, teeth, lips, nose, paranasal sinuses, pharynx (throat), trachea (wind pipe) and lungs.

130. Trachea

The trachea or wind pipe extends from the larynx. It is composed of 16-20 incomplete rings of cartilage connected with fibrous tissues. The trachea is lined by the mucous membrane. The movement of muscles in the trachea is upward; upward movement expels the inhaled dust and pollen particles. The main function of the trachea is to act as a passageway for air between the larynx and the lungs.

131. Bronchi

The wind pipe branches into two smaller tubes. These tubes are called the bronchi (in plural), or bronchus (singular). Each bronchus opens into a lung. The main function of the bronchus is to conduct air into the lungs. In lungs, the bronchus divides further into several tributaries called bronchioles, just like a branch of tree divides. No gas exchange takes place in the bronchi.

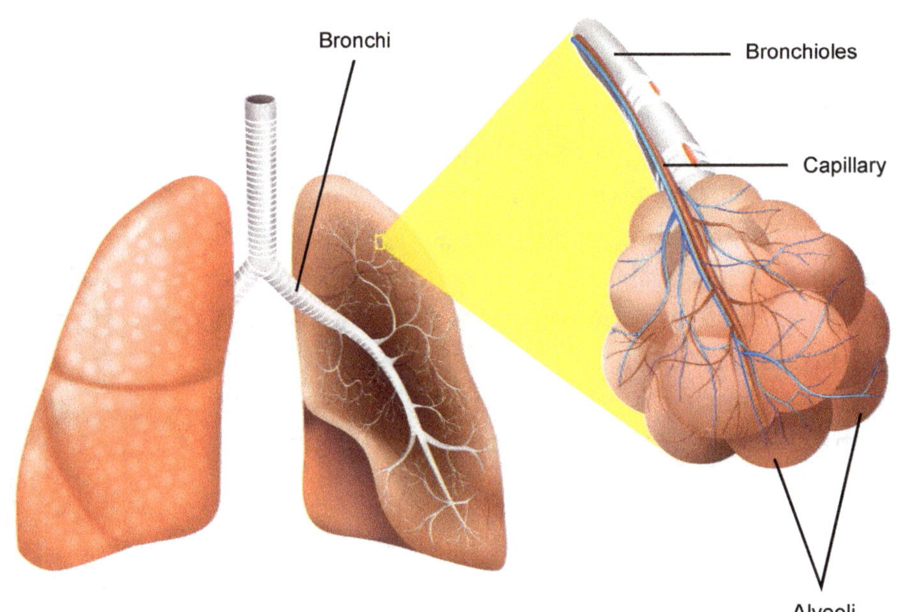

132. Alveoli

At the end of the bronchioles, there are small air sacs that are called alveoli (plural), alveolus (singular). They resemble the minute bunches of grapes. In the alveoli, blood comes in direct contact with the air. A group of capillary blood vessels surround the alveoli and the interchange of gases takes place. Overall, in alveoli, oxygen passes into the bloodstream for circulation around the body and waste carbon dioxide leaves the blood to be discharged in exhaled air.

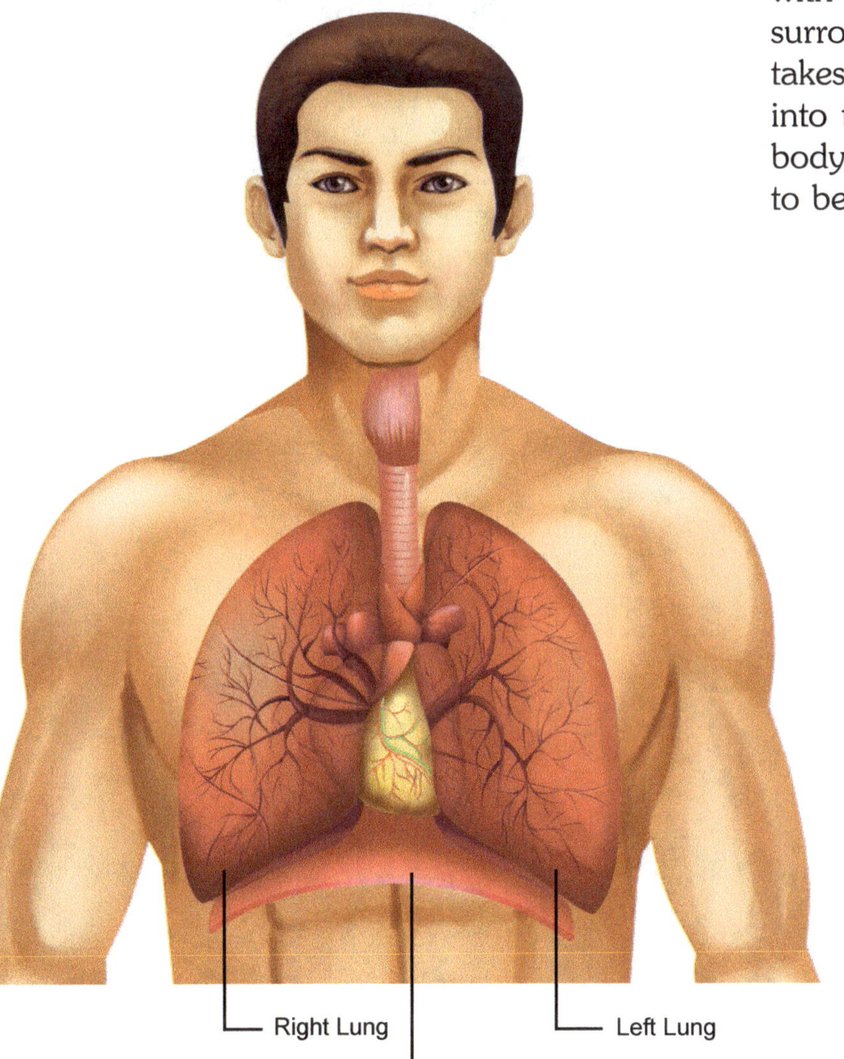

133. Lungs

The lungs are the principal organs of respiration. A human body has a pair of lung present inside the rib cage above an arched muscle called the diaphragm. The lungs are covered by two thin membranes called pleura. The lungs are cone-shaped organs with spongy texture. This spongy texture helps in the incorporation of inhaled oxygen into the blood. The lungs fill up with air. Hence, the main function of the lungs is the interchange of the gases, oxygen and carbon dioxide.

134. Pleura

Each lung is surrounded by a double serous membrane, the pleura. The part of the pleura covering each lung is called the visceral pleura. The pleura lining the ribs, is the parietal pleura. With each breath, the lungs expand and contract. The whole inner lining that covers the lungs and the ribs secretes mucus which maintains a smooth surface. This smooth, well-lubricated surface helps in easy expansion and contraction of lungs and movement of ribs.

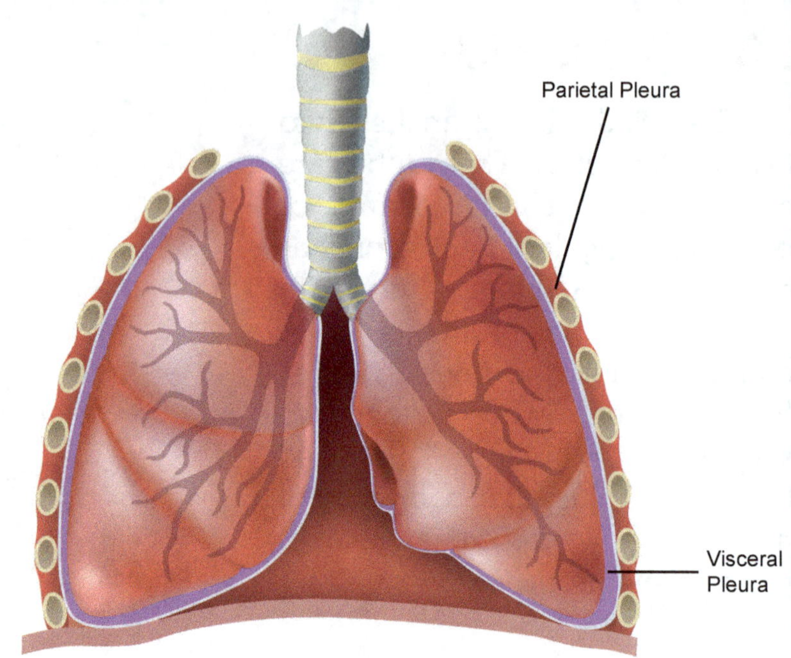

Lungs

Inhalation (Diaphragm Flattens)

Expiration (Diaphragm Relaxes)

135. Diaphragm

An arched muscle separating thoracic cavity (chest region) from the abdominal cavity, located below the lungs, is called the diaphragm. It helps in respiration process. During breathing in the diaphragm flattens while during breathing out the diaphragm relaxes and becomes arched again. The diaphragm also compresses the abdominal cavity when the inhalation of oxygen occurs.

Asthma in Respiratory System

Asthma is a disease which makes breathing difficult. Asthma attacks all age-groups but often starts in childhood. The main reason behind asthma is inflammation in air passages that carry air to and fro from the lungs. These inflammations make the airways narrower. Due to the narrow airways, less air can pass through them, which in turn causes difficulty in breathing.

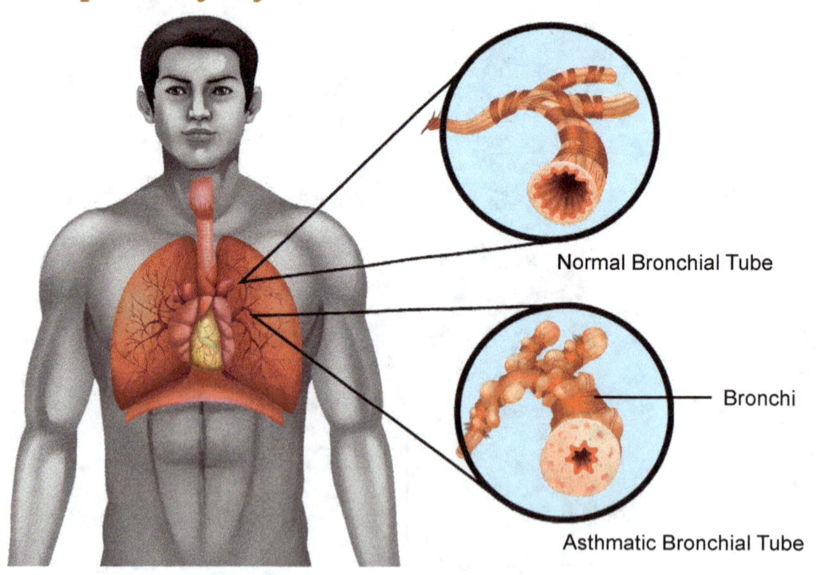

Respiration is a process in which oxygen is taken in and carbon dioxide is given out of the body. The cells use oxygen to produce energy and carbon dioxide is generated in the process. The human lung is the main organ in the respiratory system, which performs two important functions: inhalation and exhalation.

The whole process can be described as follows:

(1) When we breathe in, the air enters our nose and passed into the nasal cavity. From there, it moves to our wind pipe, which then divides into two tubes called the bronchi.

(2) The bronchi open into lungs, where they divide and branch into numerous fine tubes, each ending in an air-sac.

(3) The air-sac is called alveoli, which is a spongy perforated body, through which blood and air pass over each other and exchange of gases takes place.

(4) The oxygen is able to pass through the thin walls of the air-sacs into the blood vessels in the lungs, and then in the rest of the body, where it is used up by all the cells.

(5) On the other hand, carbon dioxide from the blood is passed into the air-sacs, from where it is breathed out of the body.

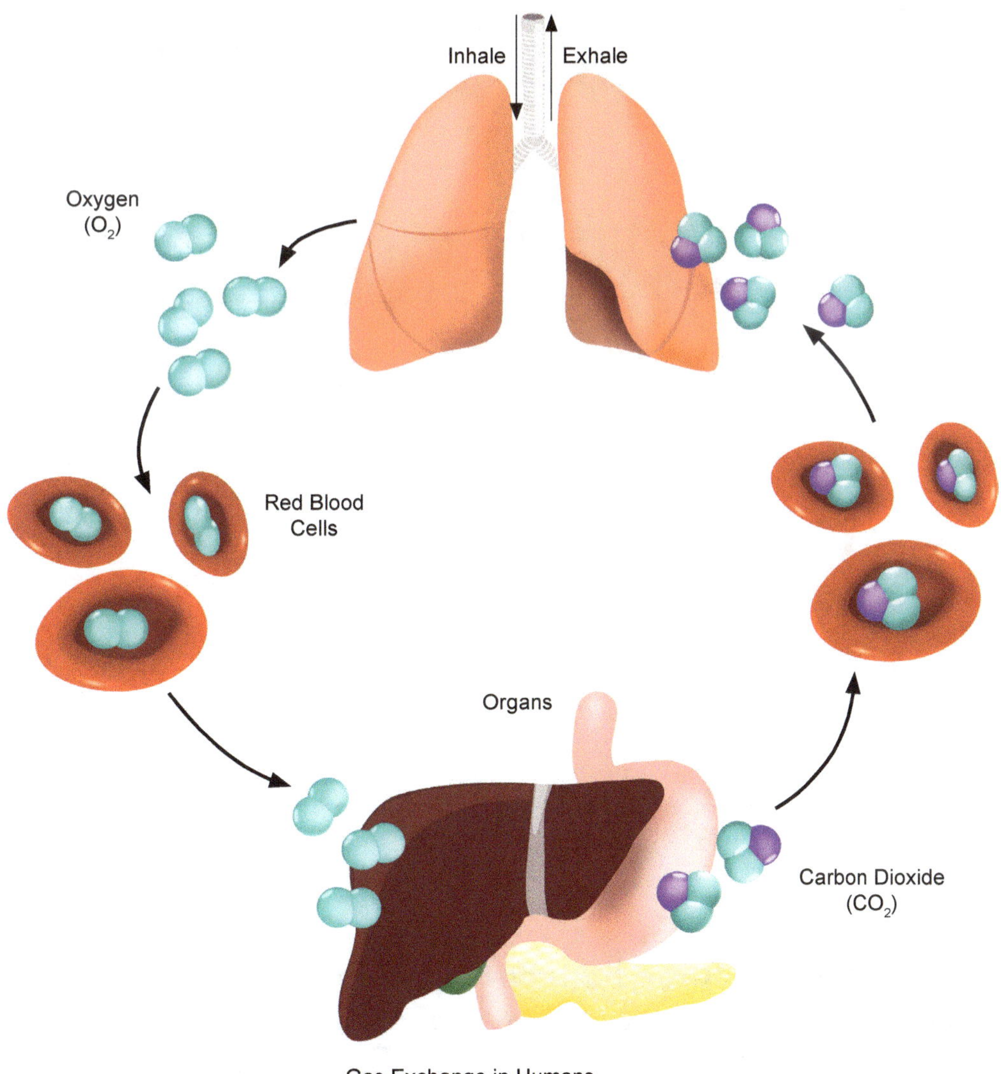

Gas Exchange in Humans

136. Endocrine System

The endocrine system is a series of glands that are spread throughout the body. These glands secrete regulatory chemicals called hormones or chemical messengers that control bodily functions. So, in short, the endocrine system is a collection of glands that control the various functions of the human body by secreting hormones. Hormone is the main regulatory unit for several bodily functions like metabolism, growth and development, tissue function, reproduction, sleep, etc.

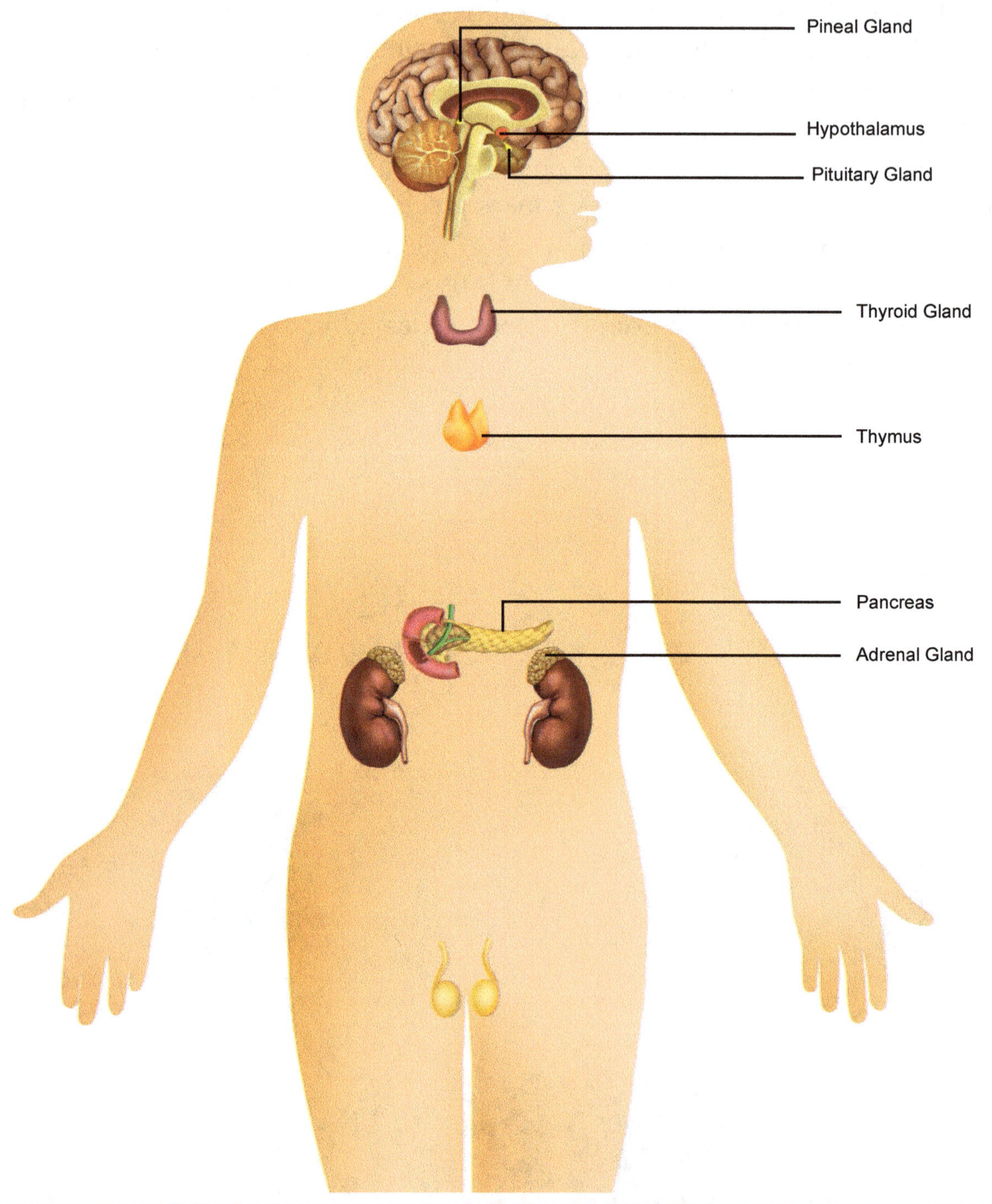

A gland is an organ that produces hormones. Glands are of two types: exocrine and endocrine. The exocrine gland secretes components through a duct directly on the site of need. For example: salivary gland and sweat gland. Endocrine glands secrete components into the bloodstream through which these chemical components are transported to the site of need (other parts of the body away from the location of the gland).

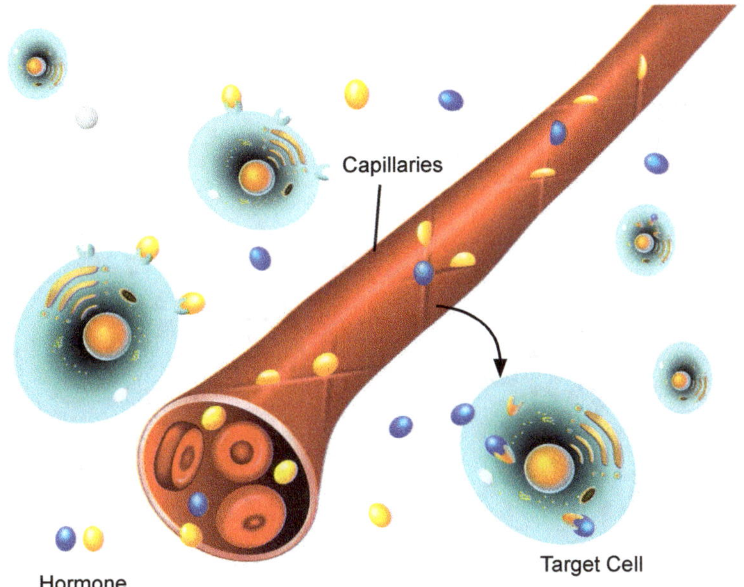

137. Hormone

Hormones are chemicals that are secreted in small amounts in one part of the body (endocrine gland) and then they travel through the bloodstream to control the activity of some other part of the body (target cell). The glands that produce hormones are principally controlled by the brain. Hormones speed up or slow down or alter the activity of those organs. There are more than 50 different hormones secreted in the human body. Some of the commonly known hormones are: insulin, thyroxine, growth hormone, etc.

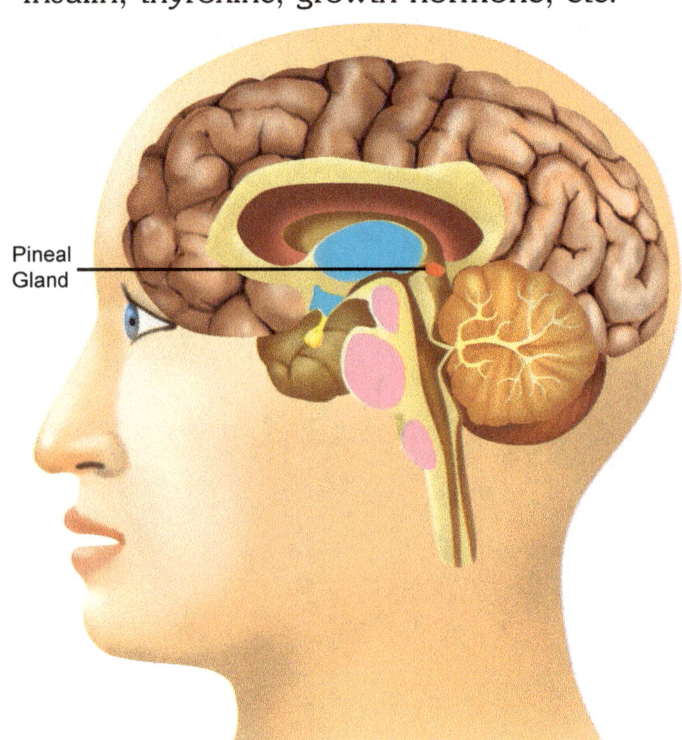

138. Pineal Gland

The pineal gland is a small endocrine gland situated in the upper part of the brain. It looks like pine cone (name derived from the Latin word pinea) and is red in colour. It secretes a hormone called melatonin. Melatonin controls the skin colouration and affects the reproductive process.

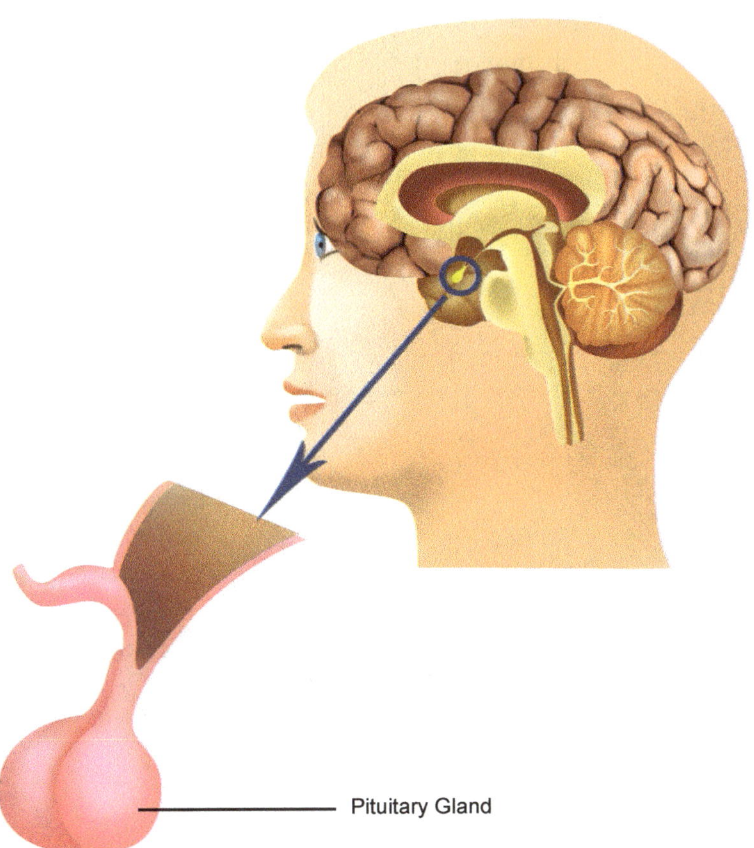

139. Pituitary Gland

The pituitary gland is a pea-sized gland that lies at the base of the skull, in the brain. It is considered as the master gland because it produces hormones that regulate hormones produced by other glands and exerts considerable control over the various bodily functions. The gland produces various hormones as–anti diuretic hormone (ADH), growth hormone, follicle stimulating hormone (FSH), leutinizing hormone (LH) and thyroid stimulating hormone (TSH). They regulate the various functions of the body. For example: bone and muscle growth, body changes at puberty, childbirth, lactation and water retention in the kidneys.

140. Thyroid Gland

The thyroid gland is located just below the larynx. The principal hormone secreted by this gland is the thyroxine hormone which regulates the metabolism in the human body, such as maintaining normal blood pressure, heart rate, digestion, muscle tone and reproductive functions. The thyroid gland plays a vital role in the growth of bones and development of the brain and nervous system in children. When the secretion of thyroxin is low, it leads to a condition called cretinism which lowers the rate of metabolism and causes the retardation of growth. Deficiency of thyroxin leads to one more hormonal disorder called hypothyroidism.

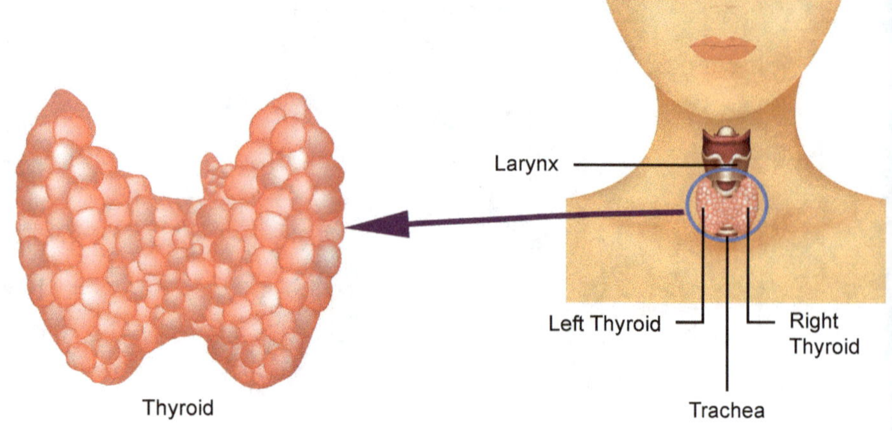

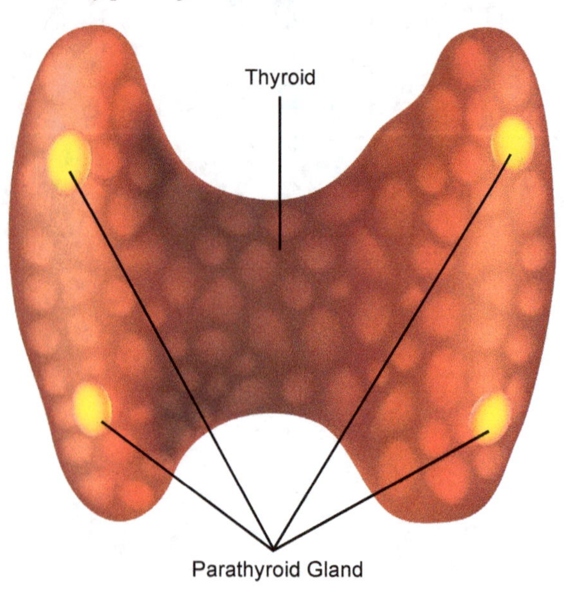

141. Parathyroid Gland

The parathyroid glands are four small glands placed two on each side of the thyroid gland in the neck. The hormone secreted by the parathyroid gland is parathormone which controls the amount of calcium in blood and bone. Over-secretion of parathormone causes calcium and phosphorous depletion from the bones and the teeth, and increase in blood calcium levels. Deficiency of parathormone lowers the blood calcium and leads to the poor development of bones in young people.

142. Thymus Gland

The pinkish-grey coloured gland located at the upper part of the chest is the thymus gland. It is one of the main organs of the immune system. At birth, this gland is quite small but as growth progresses its size increases. It grows till a person attains puberty and then it shrinks again. Its functions are not much explored, but studies suggest that the thymus gland promotes the development of specific cells of the immune system called T-lymphocytes that protect the body against bacteria and viruses. It also accelerates metabolism and speeds up growth.

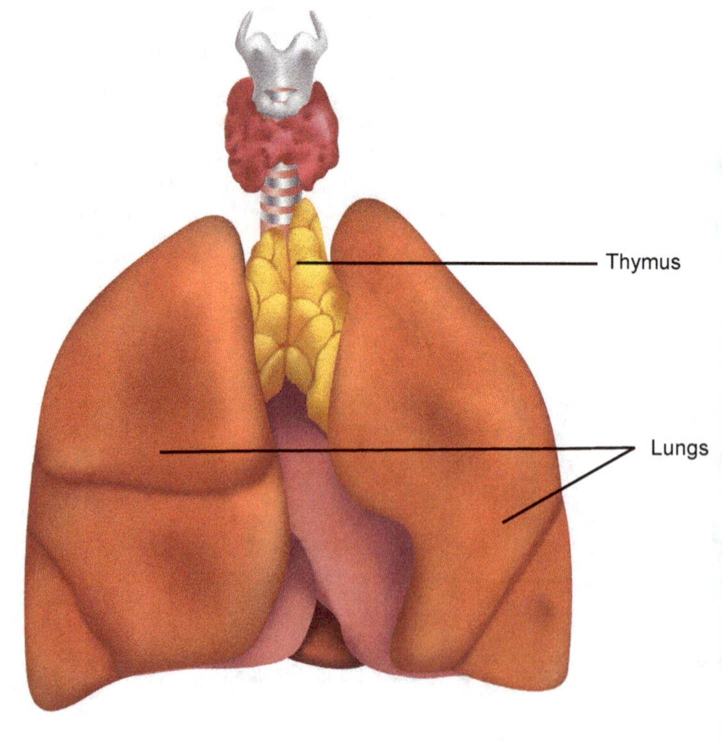

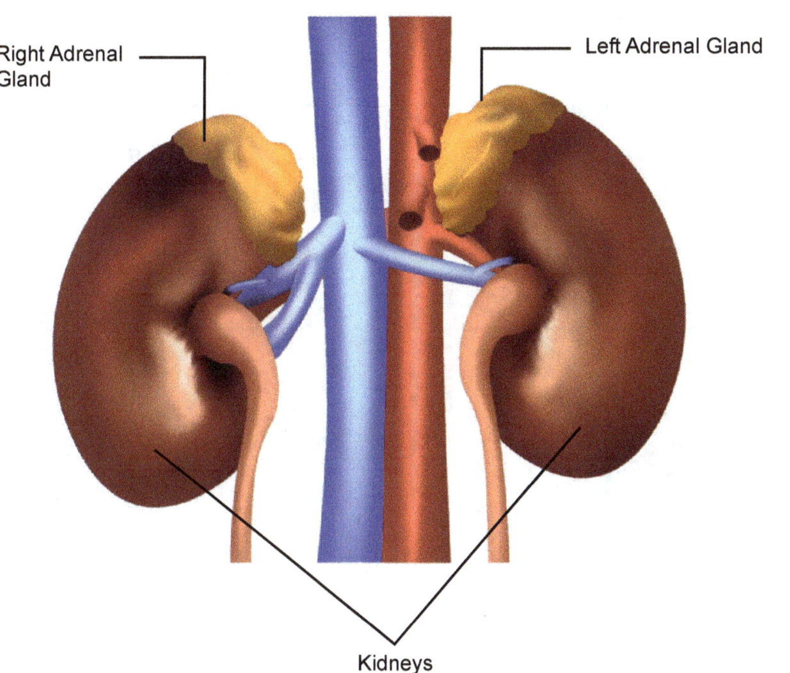

143. Adrenal Glands

The adrenal glands are located on the upper part of each kidney. The adrenal glands consist of an outer part and inner part. The outer part is called the cortex, and the inner part is called medulla. The cortex secrets a group of hormones called cortin, and the medulla secrets a hormone called adrenalin. Cortin maintains a balance between salts in the blood and those in the bones. Medulla regulates the blood pressure and the tone of involuntary muscles.

144. Islets of Langerhans

The islets of Langerhans are the endocrine part of the pancreas. These are the clusters of prism-shaped cells that release a hormone known as insulin which is required for the conversion of excess sugars into glycogen in the liver and muscles. Another hormone released by this gland is glucagon which is an antagonist of insulin. It activates liver glycogenolysis (breakdown of glycogen) and increases blood sugar level. Deficiency of insulin leads to one of the most common hormonal disorders called diabetes mellitus.

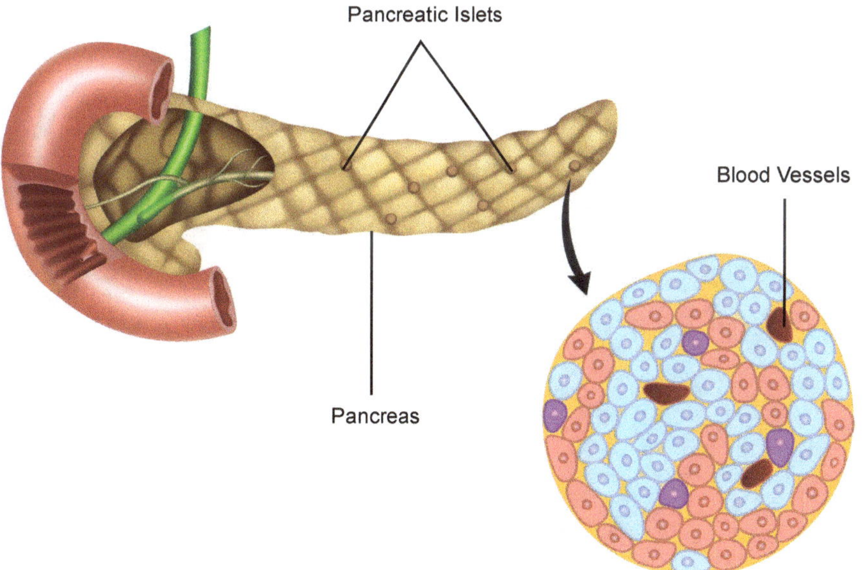

Kidney transplant is a process in which a healthy kidney is transferred from one person (donor) to another person (recipient), who has little or no kidney function. Every person has a pair of kidneys. Even if a healthy person donates one of his kidneys, he may lead a normal life as a healthy person needs only one kidney to survive. This kind of donation is known as living donation.

A patient can receive a kidney from:

- **Relatives such as a parent, sibling, or child**
- **People like friends or spouse**
- **A healthy person who has recently died and had no chronic kidney disease**

145. Excretory System

The excretory system is an organ system that helps eliminate the liquid waste from the body. This organ system consists of the following organs: a pair of kidneys, ureter, bladder and urethra. Each organ of this system performs a specific task. The kidneys form the liquid waste (urine) by filtration of plasma. The ureter carries urine from the kidneys to the bladder and the urinary bladder acts as a storage tank for the urine. Urethra, the last part of the urinary system, expels urine from the bladder.

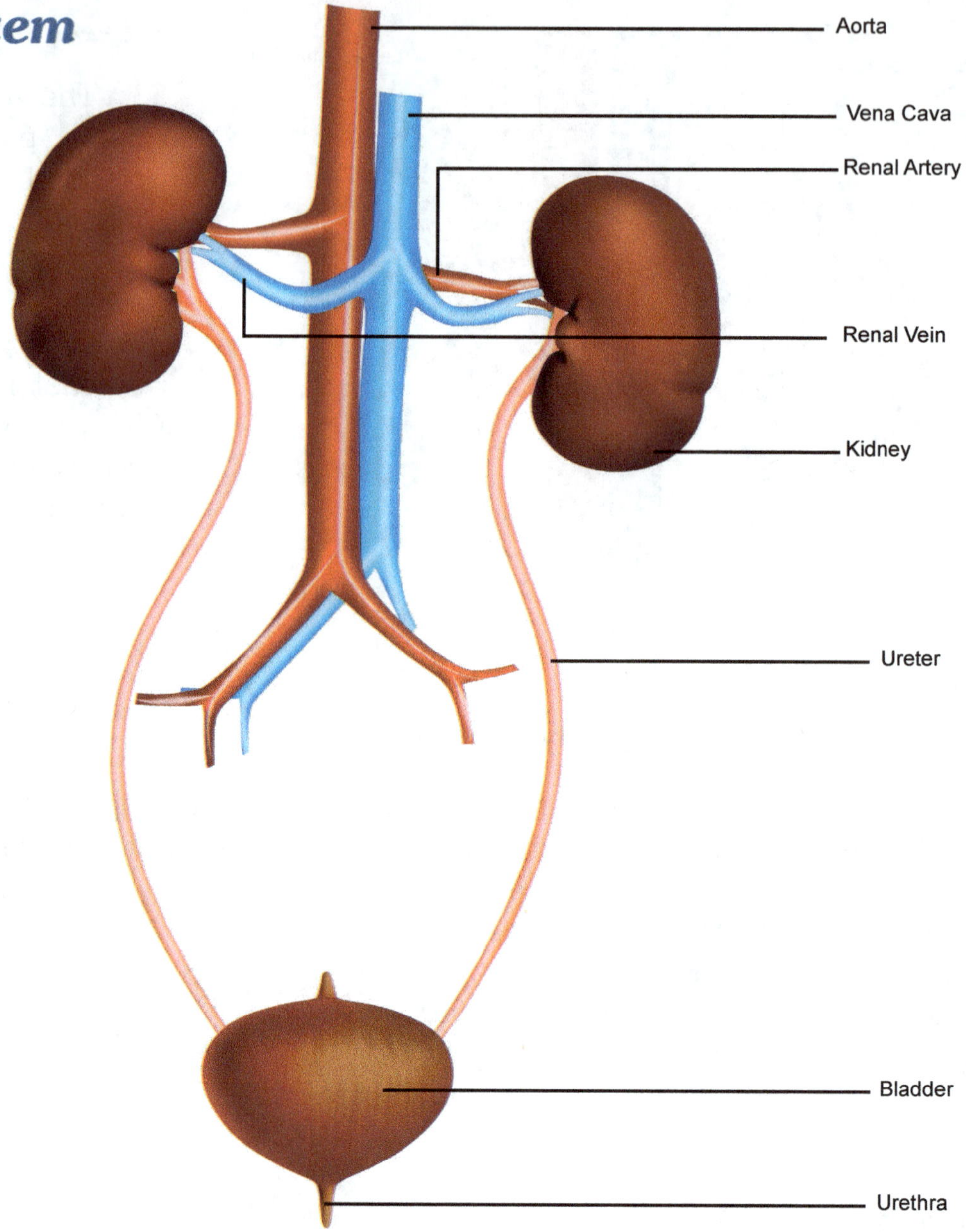

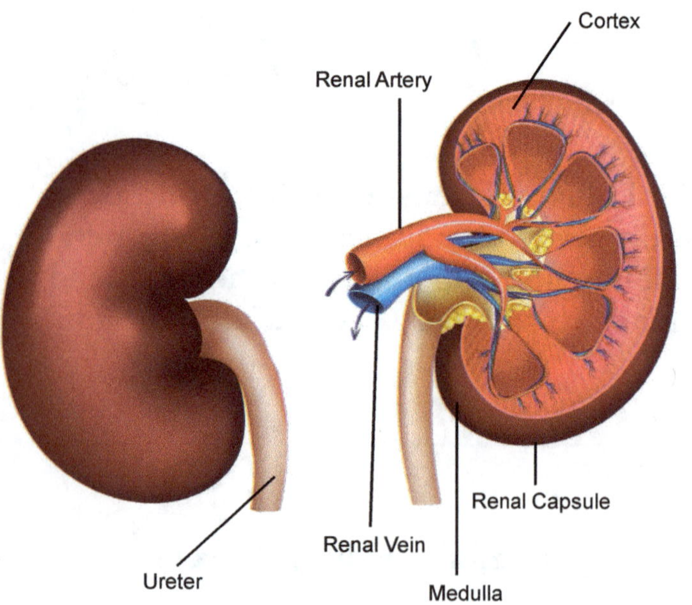

146. Kidney

Kidneys are dark reddish-brown coloured, bean-shaped organs of the excretory system, located in the back of the abdomen. Kidneys filter liquid waste and work as a disposal system of the body. Each kidney is connected with a renal artery and a renal vein. Nephrons are the basic functional units of a kidney. A kidney houses a large number of nephrons (coiled tubes) in it. Kidneys also help in the regulation of water balance, concentration of salt in blood and acid-base balance, along with the formation of red blood cells.

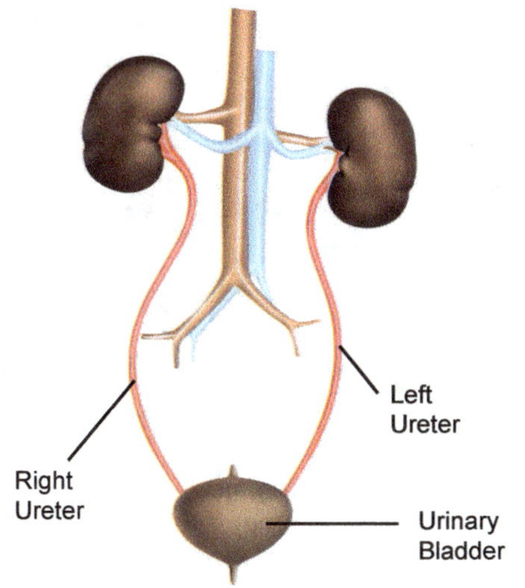

147. Ureter

The ureter is hollow tube-like structure which makes a bridge between the kidney and the urinary bladder. Each kidney is connected with a ureter. Ureters carry urine from the kidney to the urinary bladder. The length of the ureter ranges from 10-12 inches. Each ureter enters the bladder through a tunnel in the bladder wall, which is angled to prevent the urine from running back into the ureter when the bladder contracts.

148. Urinary Bladder

The urinary bladder is a storage organ (elastic in nature) of the excretory system of the liquid waste in the form of urine. It is located behind the pubic bone in the pelvis. The bladder muscles contract while urination. This contraction of muscles opens two sphincters or valves at the end of the bladder. Through these valves urine flows out. During pregnancy the uterus takes up significantly more space and severely limits the expansion of the urinary bladder.

149. Urethra

The urinary bladder ends into the urethra, a hollow tube. The urethra is a tube through which collected urine is passed out of the body. The opening of the urethra is kept closed by the urethral sphincter. It is a valve which is voluntarily controlled by a human being for urination. The act of passing the urine is called micturation. The act of micturation is a dual process: contraction of bladder muscles and relaxation of the sphincter muscles.

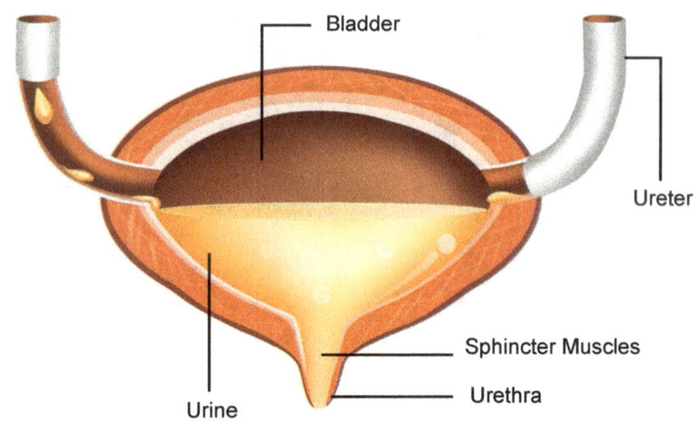

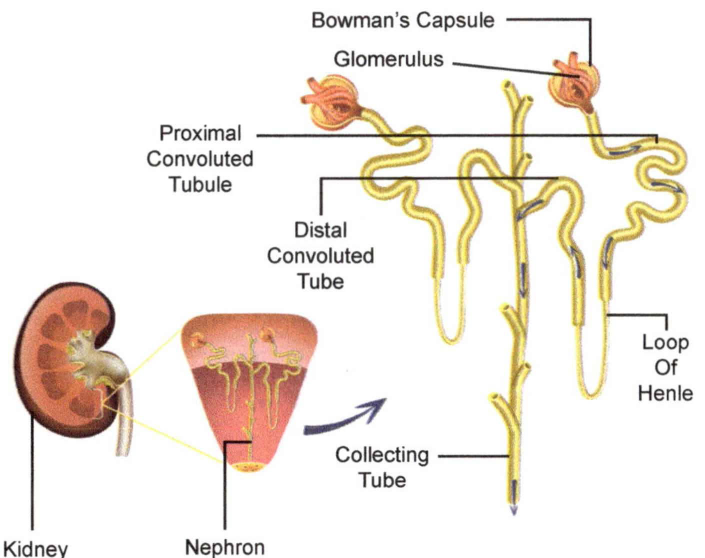

150. Nephron

A kidney consists of several excretory units, called nephrons, that work together to produce urine. They are called the filtering (functional) units of the urinary system. The main parts of the nephrons are: the glomerulus or the Malpighian body, Bowman's capsule, proximal convoluted tubule, loop of Henle, distal convoluted tube and collecting tube, which work together to filter the plasma that enters the nephrons through the blood vessels. The chemical processes through which filtration takes place are: osmosis, passive diffusion and active transport of molecules.

151. Renal Blood Vessels

The kidneys are connected with two major blood vessels: the renal artery and the renal vein. In the kidney, the renal arteries divide into several arterioles. These arterioles form a mesh-like network in the glomerulus. The blood under high pressure enters this network and is filtered through the capillary network of the glomerulus. These capillaries join together and form the renal vein which collects the filtered blood and returns it to the heart.

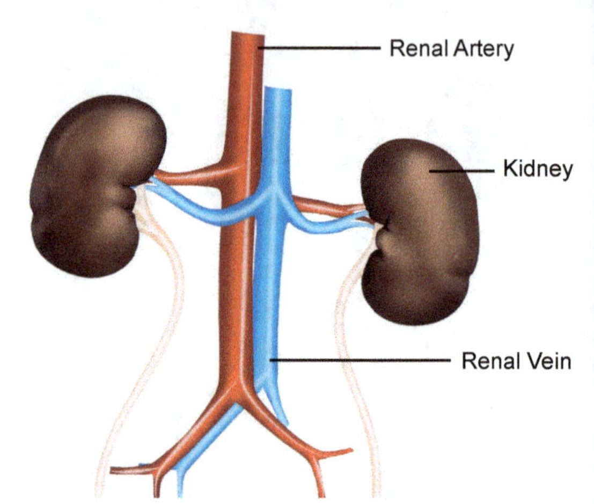

152. Glomerulus

The part of nephrons in which the blood plasma is filtered is the glomerulus which is also called Malpighian body. It is a network of capillaries. These capillaries are an extension of the renal artery. The blood plasma is forced into this capillary network under high pressure for filtration. The rate at which blood is filtered in the glomeruli is termed as glomerular filtration rate or the GFR which is an important parameter to examine the functioning of kidneys.

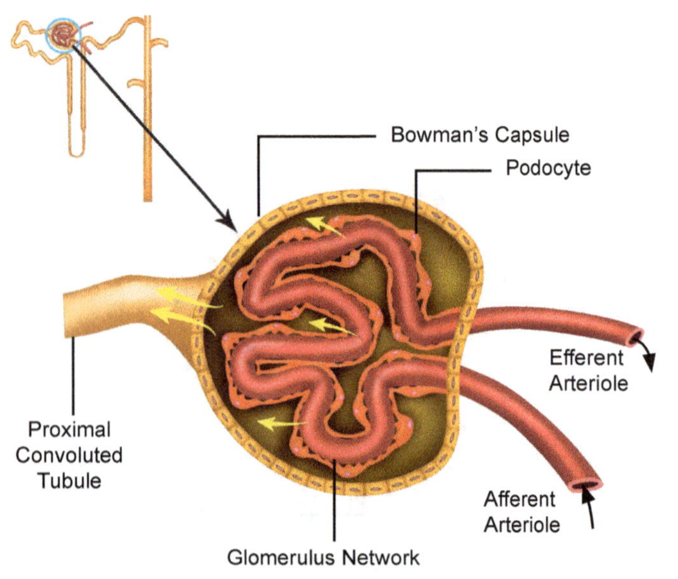

153. Bowman's Capsule

The glomerular network is enclosed in a sac-like structure known as Bowman's capsule. The Bowman's capsule is made up of specialised cells called the podocytes. The plasma after passing through the glomerulus enters the podocytes where water and dissolved substances such as sodium and glucose, pass through and travel further in the nephrons. The larger molecules and the blood cells are filtered out in the Bowman's capsule and only the smaller particles pass through.

154. Nephron Tubules

The Bowman's capsule extends into nephron tubule. There are four main tubules: the proximal convoluted tubule (PCT), the loop of Henle, the distal convoluted tubule (DCT) and the collecting tube. The tubules are the site for extensive re-absorption of useful plasma solutes. The useful solutes include: sugars and sodium; part of water is also reabsorbed back. This reabsorption is controlled by hormones. The main solute that is reabsorped back is sodium, whose reabsorption is important for the regulation of the concentration of salt in blood.

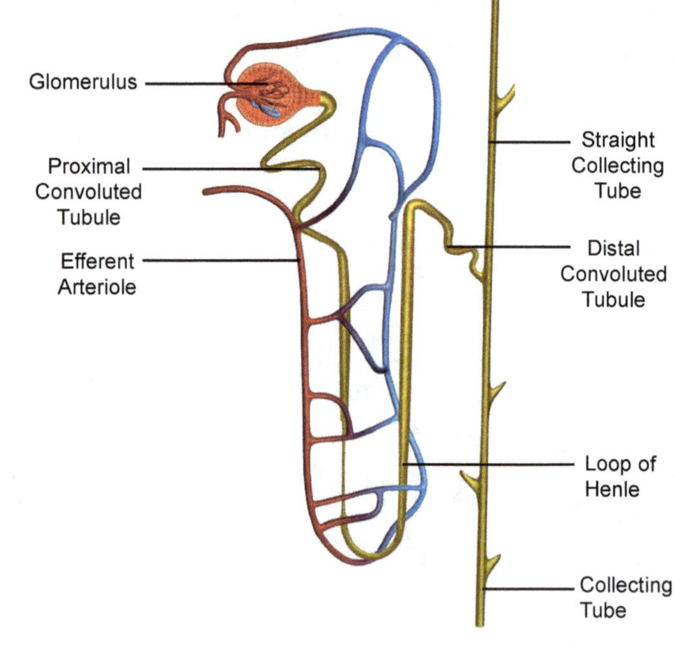

Disposal of waste products is an essential activity of living organisms. In the process of excretion waste products (mainly in chemical form: Urea) in liquid form are excreted out of the body. The three main steps involved in the formation of urine are: filtration of the plasma, reabsorption of materials/useful solutes, formation of urine and excretion of urine.

1. Renal arteries carry the impure blood plasma to the kidney, from where, tiny afferent arterioles carry blood to the Bowman's Capsules of nephrons. From here, the wastes are taken out of the blood by pressure filtration. The purified deoxygenated blood returns to heart through renal veins.

2. Essential solutes, sugar and water are reabsorbed back in the nephron tubules (the basic functional unit of kidney) from the impure liquid. The remaining liquid (urine) mostly consists of water, urea, salts and pigment.

3. The urine thus formed travels through the ureter, the urinary bladder and the urethra, and is finally excreted out of the body.

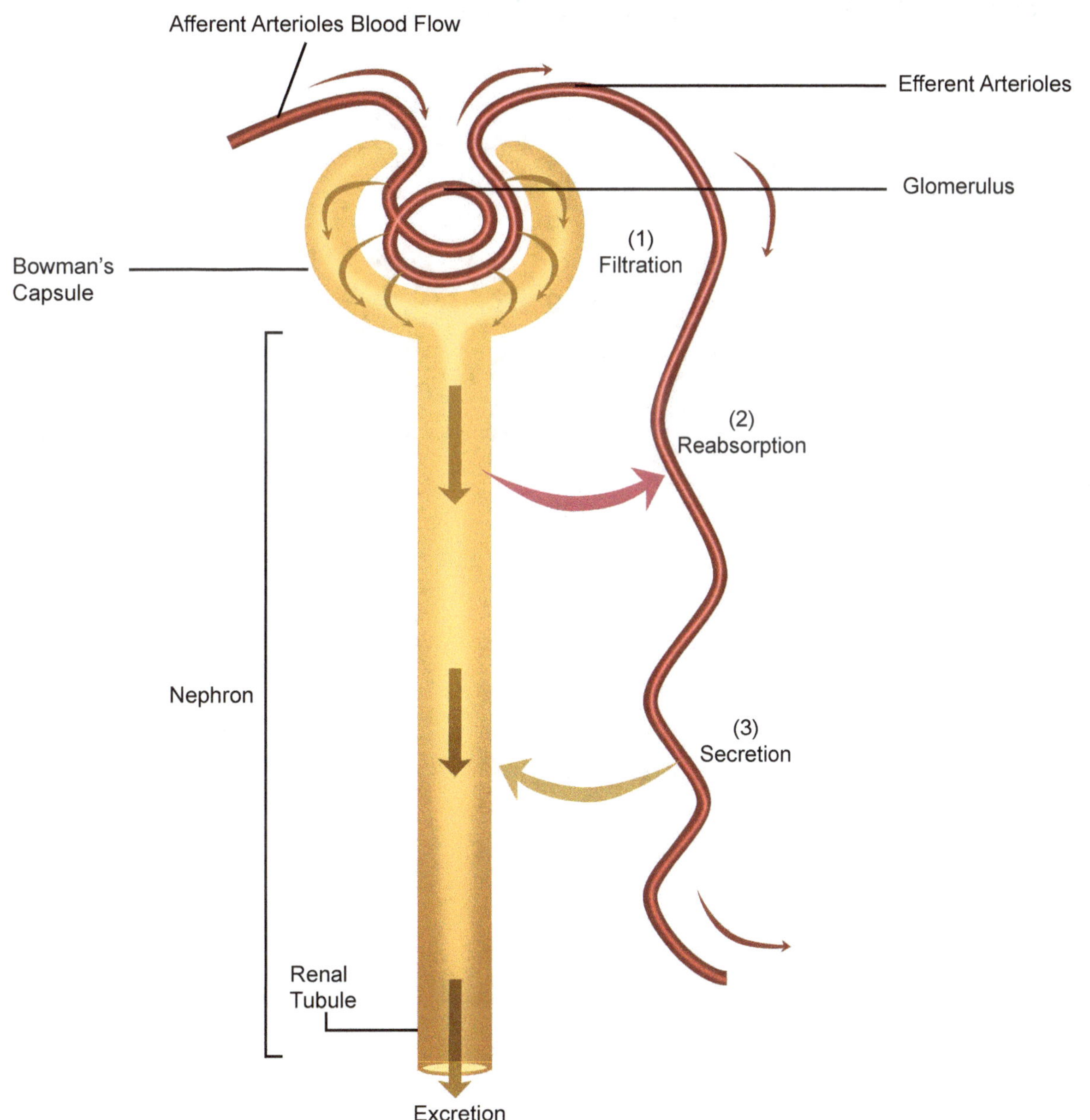

155. Reproductive System

Reproduction is the main link in the cycle of life. The lifecycle involves: birth, growth, generation of new life, ageing and death. The ability to generate a new life-form is called reproduction. The human reproductive system is a set of organs working together to produce live offspring. This system is also called the genital system. The reproductive system includes: male sex organs and female sex organs. There is a significant difference between the male and the female reproductive system and their functioning.

156. Female Reproductive Organs

The female reproductive system is a set-up that receives genetic material (sperm cells) from the male through the vagina. The sperm cells fertilise the female cells (ova) and the fertilised ovum moves in the uterus and gets embedded in the walls of the uterus. The growth of the fertilised ova takes place in the uterus in about 280 days. The fully developed human being is born through the vagina. The other major organs involved are: fallopian tubes and ovaries.

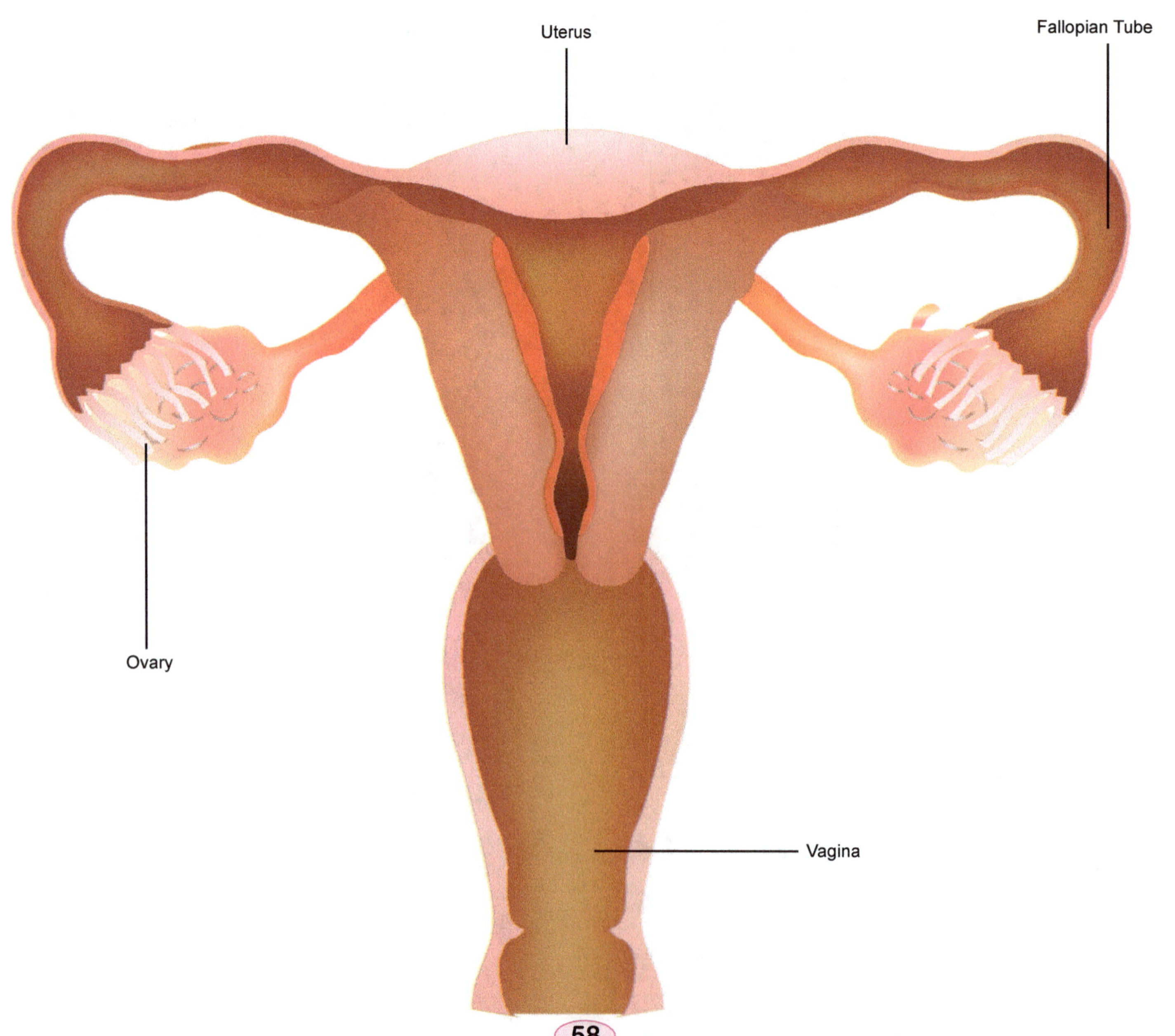

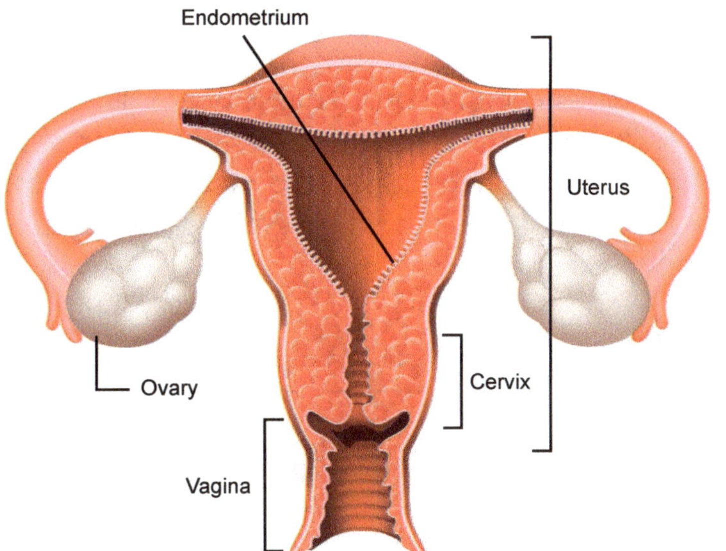

157. Vagina and Uterus

Vagina is an interface between the external and internal reproductive organs. The external organs include: vulva, clitoris and vestibule. It is a muscular tube which is connected with blood vessels and nerves. It makes the connection between the vestibule and the uterus. Uterus is a pear-shaped organ which is the house where a fertilised ovum is embedded. It is situated behind the rectum. The internal lining of the uterus is called the endometrium which receives the fertilised ovum.

158. Ovaries

Ovaries are glands that generate ova or eggs. A female body has a pair of almond-sized oval-shaped ovaries. The ovaries perform two main functions: they produce ova; they produce two major hormones required for reproduction, oestrogen and progesterone. The parent hormone that controls the hormone production of the ovaries is the gonadotrophic hormone, secreted by the anterior pituitary gland.

159. Fallopian Tube

Each ovary is connected with a narrow tube-like structure called the fallopian tube. The open end of the fallopian tubes looks like a flower sepal. These fallopian tubes are also called uterine tubes through which ova travel. The ovarian arteries supply blood to the ovaries and these tubes which are a duct and they transport ova generated by the ovaries to the interior of the uterus. Fertilisation of the male sperm cells and female ovum normally occurs in these tubes.

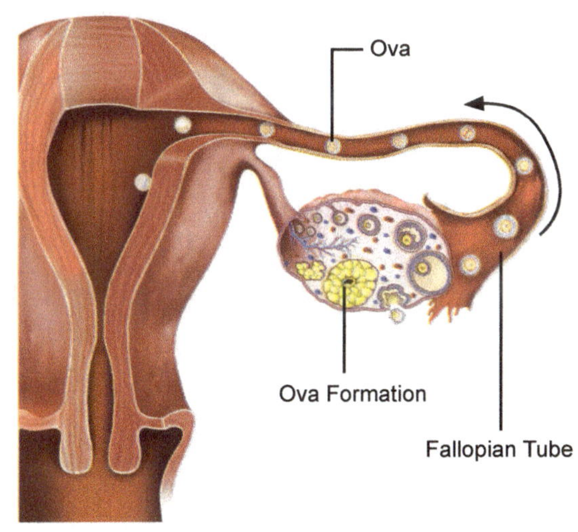

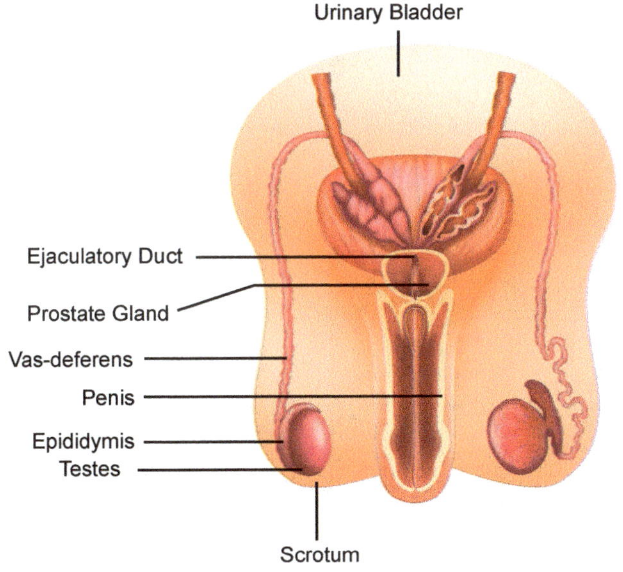

160. Male Reproductive Organs

The male reproductive system is a set of organs which produce male gametes (sperm cells) and deliver them to the uterus of the female. The primary male reproductive organs are the testicles and scrotum. The testes or testicles generate sperms. The formation of sperms is activated by the hormone testosterone (male hormone). The sperms pass from the testes into the vas deferens through the epididymis. Sperm cells are mixed with liquid in the seminal vesicles to form semen. The semen is ejaculated out of the penis.

161. Nervous System

The nervous system controls all the basic bodily functions and behaviour. That is why it is known as the principal organ system. The basic unit of the nervous system is a neuron. The two major parts of the nervous system are: the central nervous system and the peripheral nervous system. The central nervous system is comprised of the brain and the spinal cord, whereas the peripheral nervous system is comprised of the cranial nerves, spinal nerves and the visceral nerves.

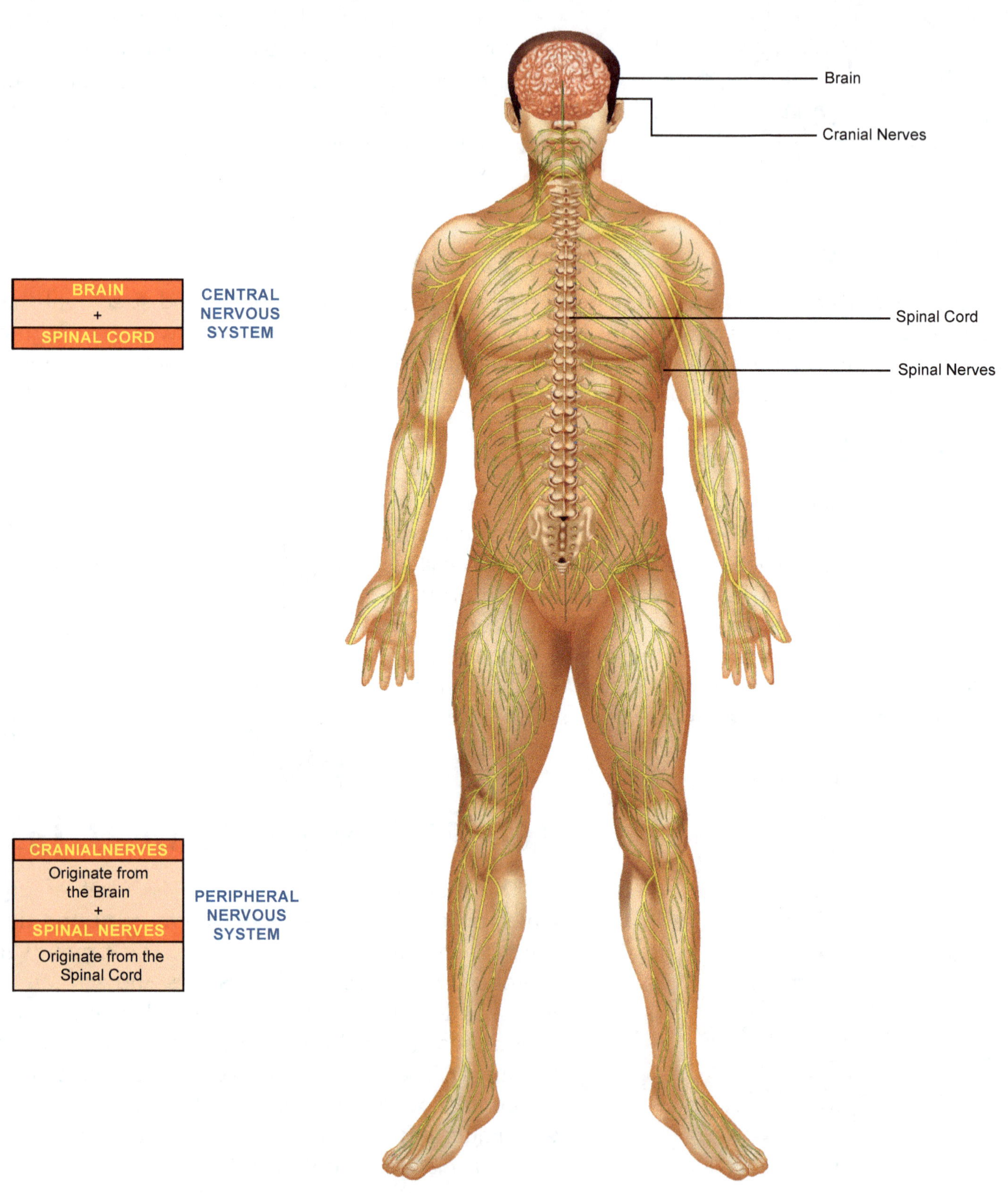

162. Neuron

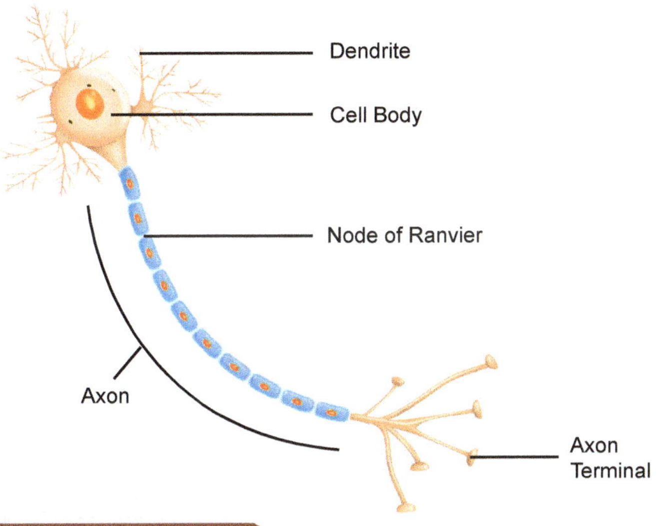

Neuron or nerve cell is the basic unit of the nervous system. Neurons act as transmitters and receptors of nerve impulses. They carry information through electrical and chemical signals. Neurons are supported by a special tissue called the neuroglia. The main components of a neuron are: dendrites, cell body, node of ranvier and axon. The axons transmit information gathered in the cell body of the neuron to the other cells. Dendrites act as antennae and receive information.

Receptors

Receptors collect impulses from the surrounding and support the transport of the impulses from the body to the central nervous system.

163. Synapse

In the nervous system, a synapse is a space between two neurons that permits a neuron (or nerve cell) to pass an electrical or chemical signal to another cell (neural or otherwise). It provides a bridge between two neighbouring neurons or between a neuron and an effector organ; nerve impulses are transmitted by a chemical neurotransmitter.

Effector Organ

Part of the body that responds to a stimulus

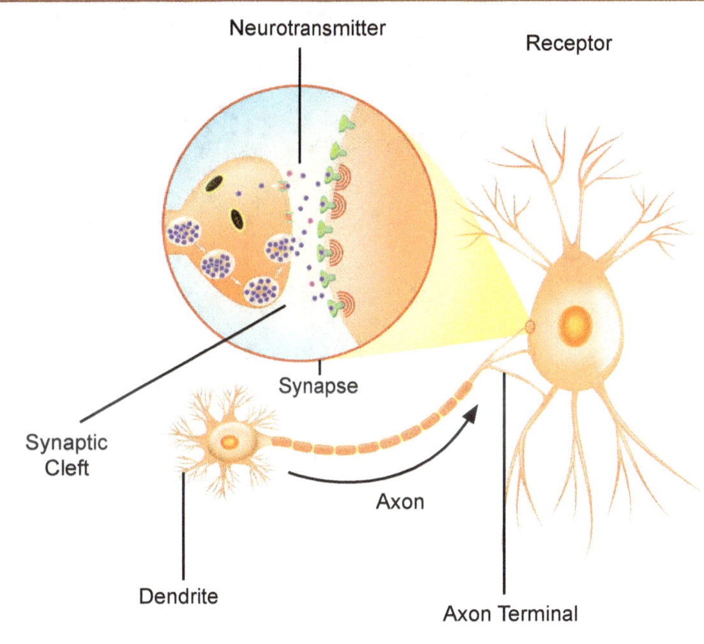

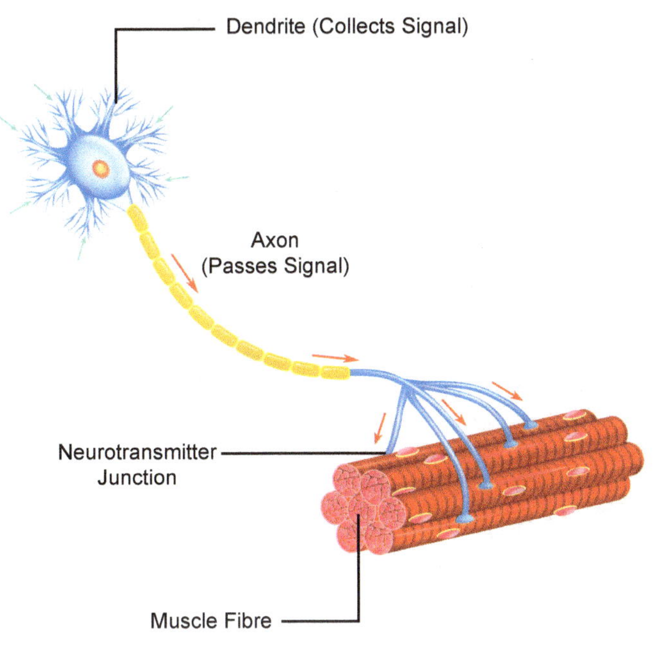

164. Motor Neuron

Motor neurons, also known as efferent neurons, are the connecting unit between the muscular system and the central nervous system. They carry information from the nervous system to the muscles. The signals are transmitted through the neurons to the effector organs where an impulse has to be generated. In case of muscles, these impulses can be relaxation and contraction and in case of glands they can be a signal to secrete hormone. Acetylcholine is a neurotransmitter that passes the impulse from a neuron to a muscle.

165. Sensory Neuron

Sensory neurons, also known as afferent neurons, carry signals from the receptor in the body towards the central nervous system. Dendrites of the sensory neurons collect the signals from the receptors in the skin, eye, nose and other sensory organs, and carry them towards the central nervous system. The stimuli are transferred to the cell body and then to the axons. These axons join with the other dendrites of the neurons and so on; this is the way sensory stimulus is transferred to the spinal cord and the brain.

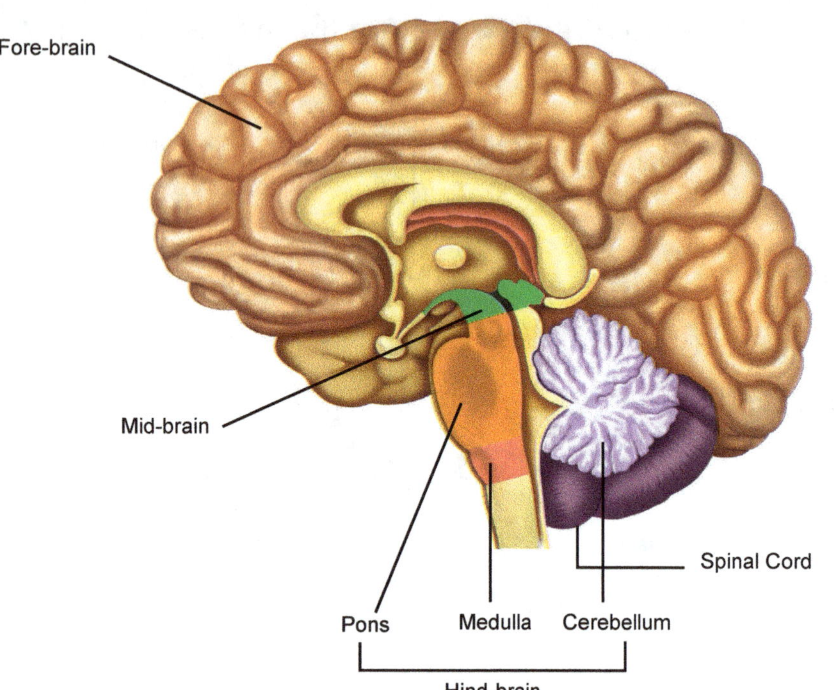

166. Brain

The brain is the central control system of the body, also called the master organ of the body. It lies in the skull (brain case) and protected by a bony box called cranium. It has three main parts: the fore-brain, mid-brain and hind-brain. The human brain works like a master computer. The brain processes the information, stores the information and responds to the information. It sends and receives messages to and from all parts of the body through neurons.

167. Fore-brain

The fore-brain or the cerebrum is the largest part of the brain and it makes about 85% of the brain. The folds in the fore-brain help it to fit into the skull. The main parts of the fore-brain are: cerebral hemispheres and basal ganglia. Cerebrum is the base of memory, intelligence and mind. It is the part which helps us to think, learn, remember, speak and feel. The cerebrum also controls body-part movements and sensory stimuli.

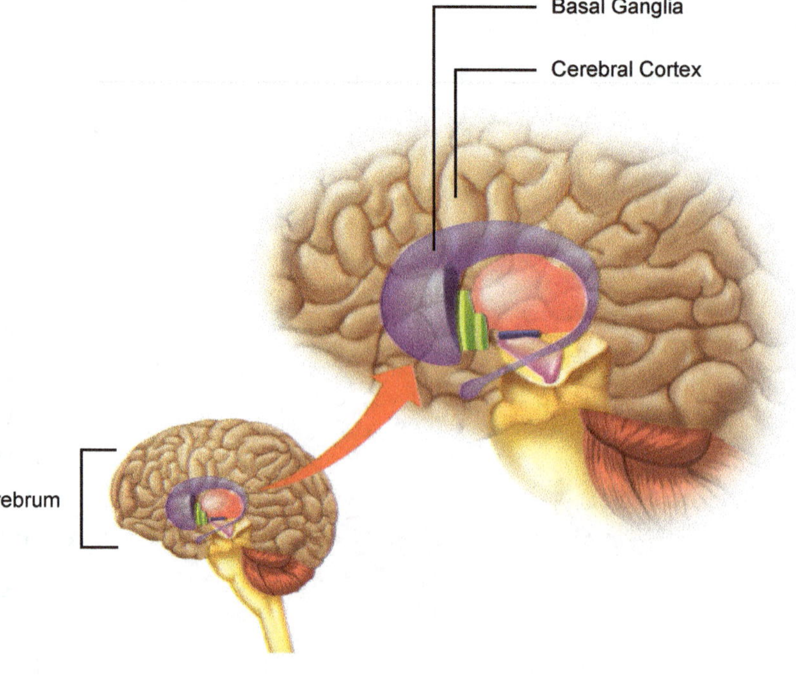

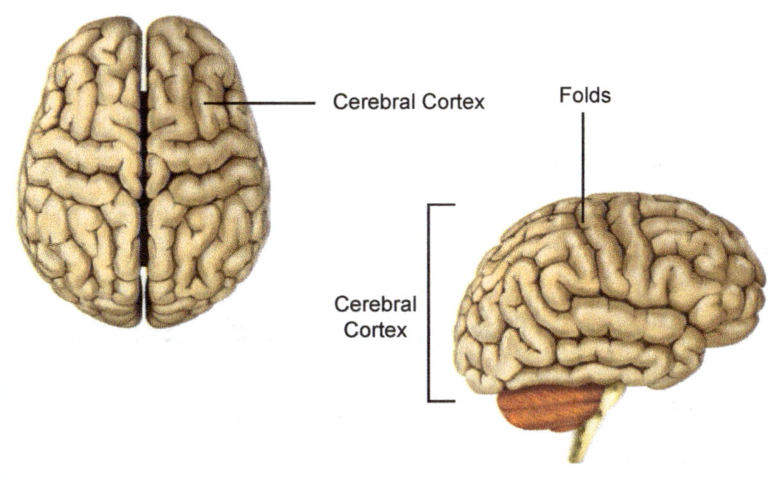

168. Cerebral Cortex

Cerebral cortex is an important region of the cerebrum; it is also known as the grey matter of the brain. Grey matter is the region where nerve cells concentrate. These nerve cells are arranged as irregular folds. These irregular folds increase the surface area of the cortex. These cells of the cortex are connected with nerve fibres which make up the white matter. The cerebral cortex is divided into two main areas: the motor area and the sensory area.

169. Thalamus

The thalamus is a large dual lobe structural part of the brain which performs endocrine function. It is located between the cerebral cortex and mid-brain or at the top of the brain-stem. It performs an important function in our body. It receives the sensory impulses and relays them to the sensory centre of the brain.

170. Hypothalamus

The hypothalamus is the principal centre of the autonomic nervous system. It is a part of the back part of the fore-brain and is located beneath the thalamus. The hormone released by the hypothalamus activates the production of other hormones by the pituitary gland, the master gland of the body.

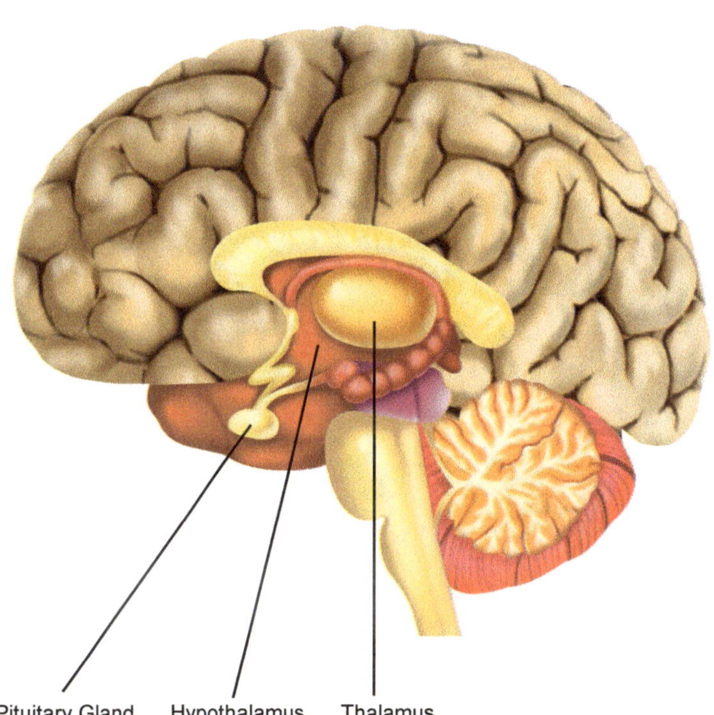

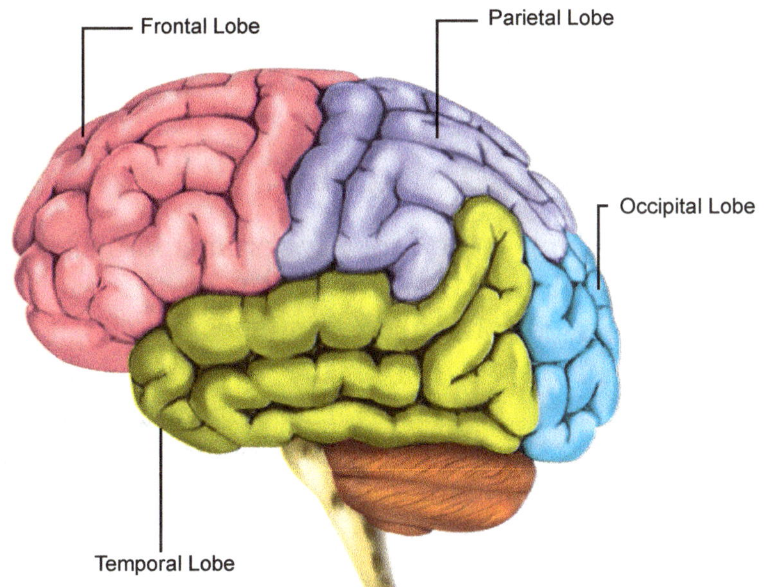

171. Lobes of Cerebrum

The cerebral hemisphere has several folds present on its surface. These folds are called cortex. These folds can be divided into four sections, called the lobes: the frontal lobe, parietal lobe, occipital lobe and temporal lobe. These lobes are the control centre of various functions. The frontal lobe controls thought and speech, the temporal lobe controls the sense of olfaction and smell, the parietal lobe controls the posture and the occipital lobe controls the vision.

172. Brain-stem

Brain-stem is a stem-like part of the brain that connects the cerebrum and the spinal cord. It usually includes the medulla oblongata, pons, and mid-brain. A pair of ten cranial nerves comes from the brain-stem. The parts of the brain-stem work together to control the movements in the body.

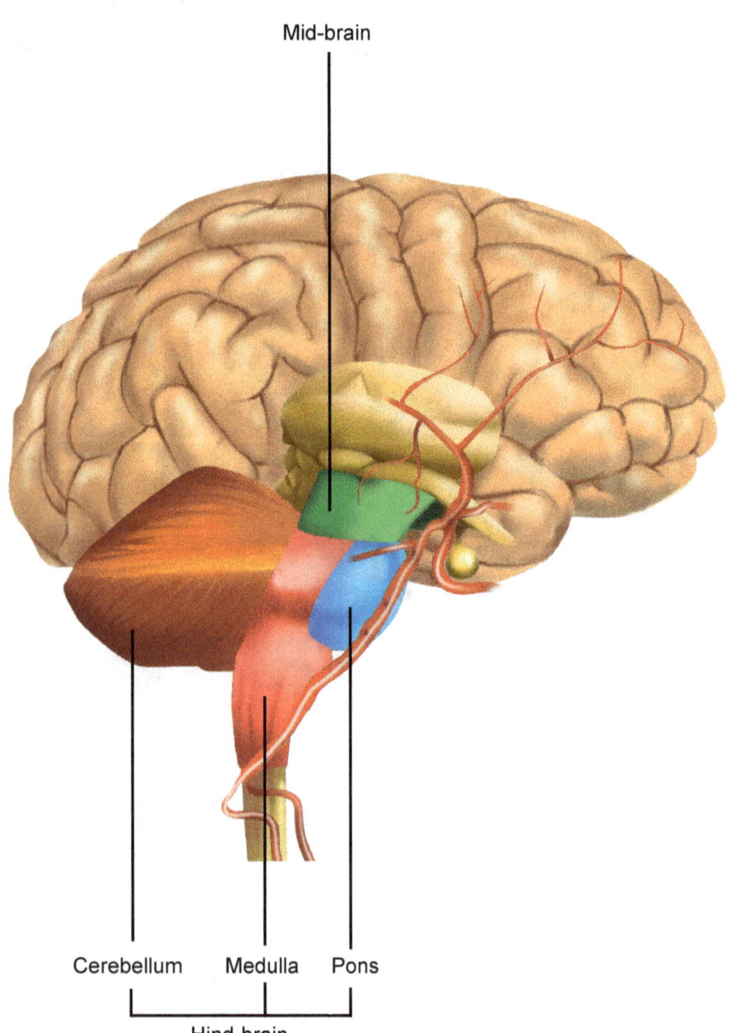

173. Mid-brain

The mid-brain is also known as mesencephalon. It is the topmost part of the brain-stem, located between fore-brain and hind-brain. It is a junction through which the nerves from the fore-brain pass towards the hind-brain (medulla and pons). The top of the mid-brain houses the sight and hearing reflex centres, through which specific signals are responded. The mid-brain also controls certain functions of the *eye* such as movement and size of the pupils.

174. Hind-brain

The hind-brain is also known as rhombencephalon. It is located below the mid-brain, made up of the pons, medulla oblongata and cerebellum. The cerebellum is the largest part of the hind-brain. One of the main functions of the hind-brain is to control breathing and coordination between muscles. It also helps in the major and complex body movements (arms and legs).

175. Pons

Pons is a large body of transverse nerve fibres. The nerve fibres of pons are the connecting mode between the brain and the cerebellum. Pons in association with the cerebellum helps maintain balance in the body. Individually, pons affects the respiratory process and the breathing.

176. Medulla Oblongata

Medulla oblongata is the lowest portion of the brain-stem. It accommodates several nuclei and cell bodies of cranial nerves. In medulla, the grey matter is inside and the white matter is exposed on the surface. Its main function is to control several functions such as breathing, heart beat rate (cardiac functions), blood pressure and peristaltic movements of the alimentary canal.

177. Cerebellum

Cerebellum is the most important part of the hind-brain, located at the base of the brain. Cerebellum is principally connected with the cerebral hemisphere and the brain-stem. It is connected with the sight reflex centres that lie in the mid-brain. The main function of the cerebellum is to coordinate muscular movements such as walking, dancing, riding a bicycle, etc. It also helps maintain posture and balance of body.

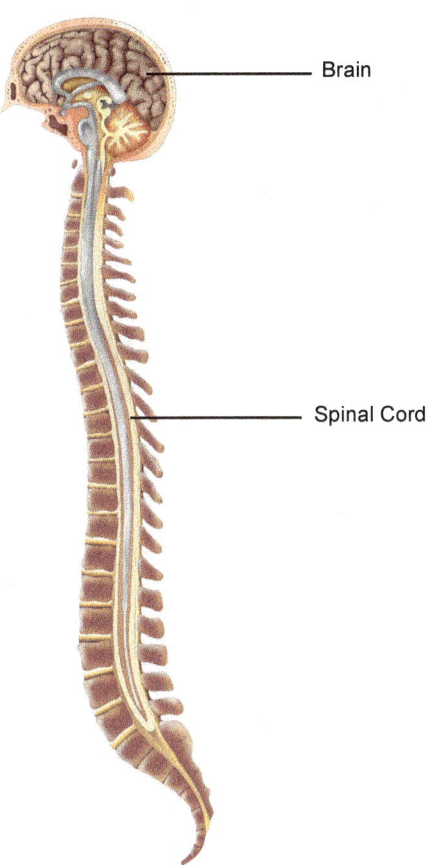

178. Central Nervous System (CNS)

The central nervous system is also called the cerebrospinal nervous system, where 'cerebro' refers to the brain and 'spinal' refers to the spinal cord. The brain and the spinal cord together weave a wide network of nerves that work day and night and keep the body functioning. The brain is said to be the main control centre of all the other organs and related stimuli. The spinal cord though being a part of skeleton is a plexus of nerves that control the entire skeletal and muscular system. The work of CNS is to direct incoming messages to the motor neurons that are connected to the part of body which will respond to a stimulus.

179. Spinal Cord

The spinal cord connects the whole body to the brain. It is the continuation of the medulla oblongata through the backbone. Several nerve fibres branch out from the spinal cord to all parts of the body. As many as 31 pairs of nerves arise from the spinal cord. Messages travel to and between the brain and the rest of the body through the spinal cord and its nerves. It also controls the reflex action.

Spinal cord is the connection between the body and the brain. Any injury to the spinal cord breaks the connection between the brain and the body. The common effects seen after spinal cord injury are: loss of movement, sensation and bowel/bladder control, exaggerated reflex actions, severe pain, etc.

180. Peripheral Nervous System (PNS)

The peripheral nervous system (PNS) is the part of the nervous system which includes the nerves and ganglia that are outside of the brain and spinal cord. It consists of 3 types of nerves: spinal nerves, cranial nerves and visceral nerves which are the connecting wires between CNS and sensory organs. The system is further divided into two sub-divisions: the somatic and autonomic nervous systems. The nerves of somatic nervous system are connected to the skeletal muscles. These nerves carry signals to the skeletal muscles from the brain. The other is the peripheral nervous system that carries signals to the glands, organs, the heart muscles and the digestive system.

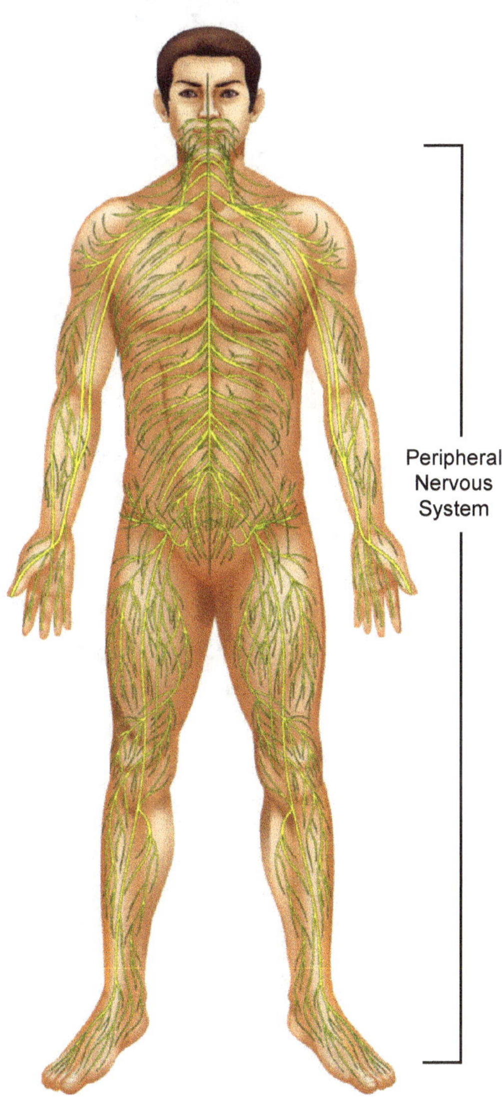

181. Somatic Nervous System

The part of the peripheral nervous system that sends motor impulses to skeletal muscles is the somatic nervous system. The sensory neurons (afferent neuron) and the motor neurons (efferent neuron) are the part of this nervous system. The main function of somatic nervous system is to exchange impulses between the central nervous system and organs, muscles and skin. This system allows us to perform various bodily movements and other voluntary functions.

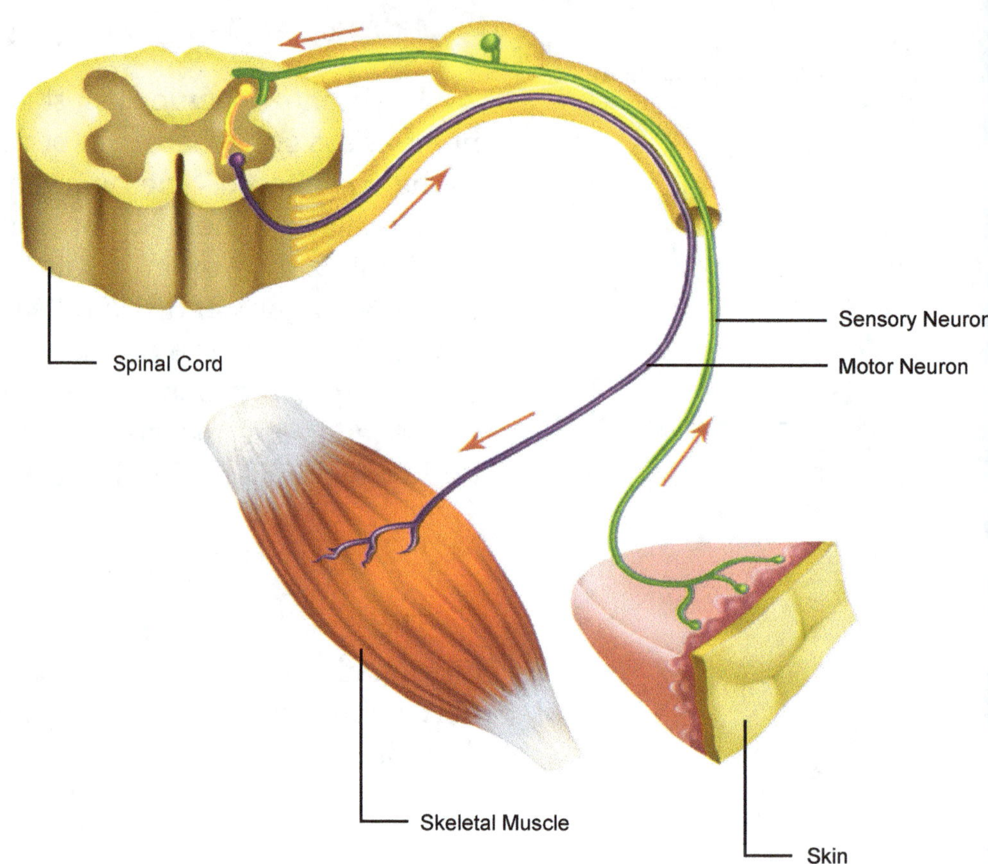

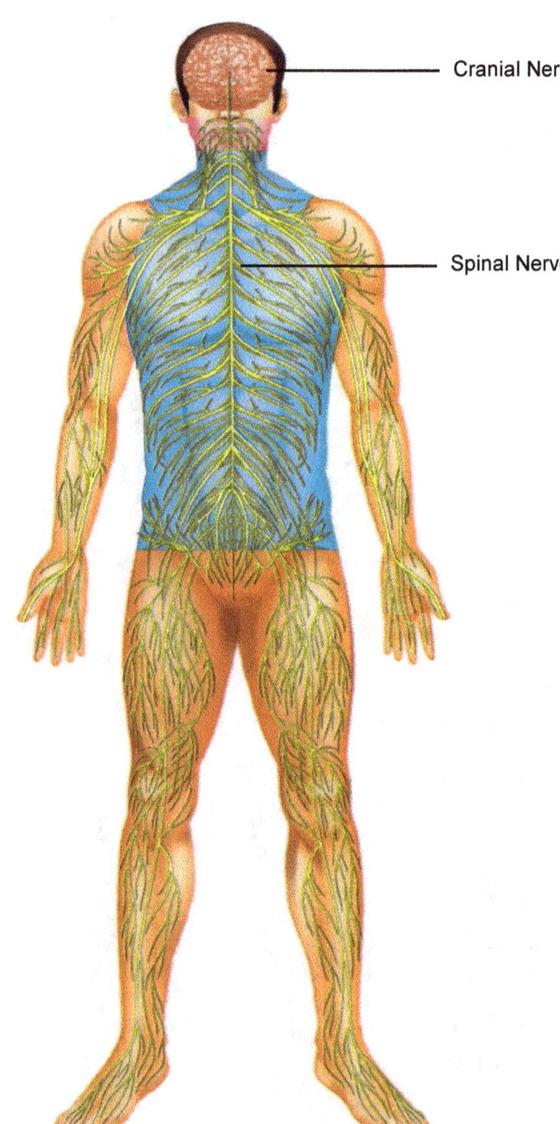

182. Spinal Nerves

The spinal nerves are part of the peripheral nervous system. These nerves arise directly from the spinal cord. There are 31 pairs of spinal nerves in the peripheral nervous system. The major function of these nerves is to exchange sensory, motor and autonomic signals between the spinal cord and the body.

183. Cranial Nerves

The cranial nerves are also the part of the peripheral nervous system. The human body has 12 pairs of cranial nerves. These arise from the brain and spread throughout the head. These are primarily connected with the head, neck and thorax areas. Cranial nerves are numbered in pairs from I to XII. The nerves, I, II and VIII carry only sensory signals to the brain; IV, VI, XI, XII carry motor messages away from the brain; and III, V, VII, IX, X are sensorimotor.

184. Autonomic Nervous System

This part of the peripheral nervous system controls the involuntary movements in the body, such as–controlling and coordinating smooth and cardiac muscle functions, and the endocrine glands. This system is further divided into the sympathetic and the parasympathetic nervous system. These two sub-divisions of autonomic system work in opposition to each other to balance the internal homeostasis of the body. The autonomic nervous system acts as the alert/warning system. It is a manager as it manages the functions of all the bodily systems.

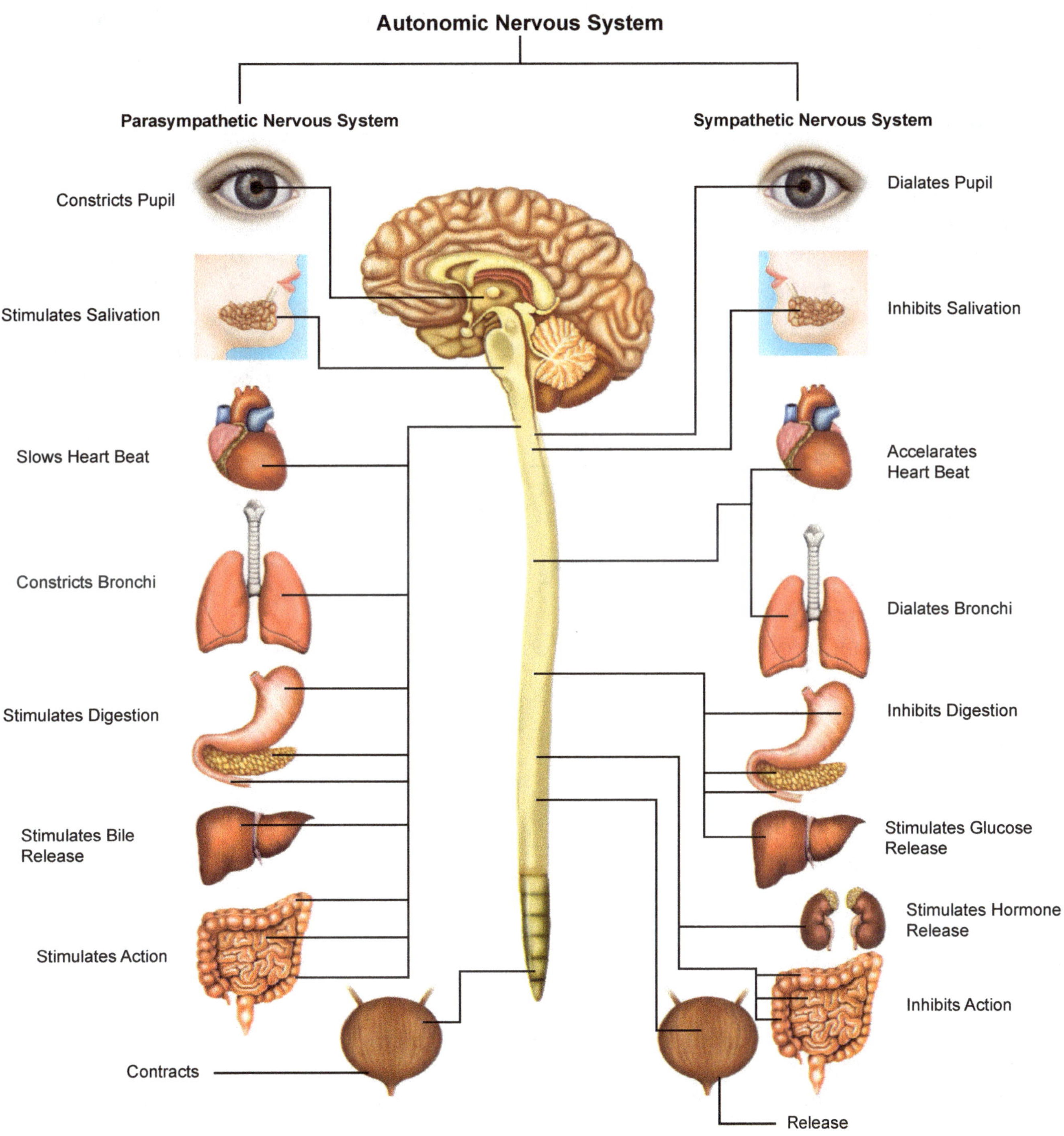

185. Parasympathetic Nervous System

The parasympathetic nervous system functions when the body is at rest. It functions totally opposite to the sympathetic system, by calming down the body. This system decreases the rate of heart beat, dilates bronchi and pupil of the eye and relaxes stomach, intestine and bladder.

186. Sympathetic Nervous System

The sympathetic nervous system stimulates the body to react in emergency conditions by regulating certain bodily functions, such as increasing the heart rate, enlarging the pupils, decreasing digestion, etc. This system prepares our body to defend itself or respond in any dangerous situation itself (fight or flight response).

Reflex Action

What is reflex action? We can understand it simply with this question. What happens when we accidently place our hand on a pin?

Answer: We move away our hand instantly.

This action, that our body performs automatically when there is an emergency is known as reflex action. It occurs quickly and unconsciously. In a reflex action, the messages are received by the spinal cord, and a quick decision is taken by the spinal cord about what to do and it quickly informs the body-part. These actions are involuntary.

In the spinal cord, the nerve impulses move from sensory neurons to the interneurons (also known as relay neurons). The impulses are then sent to motor neurons which project out of the spinal cord to stimulate your muscles (effector) in order to contract, hence snatching your hand away from the hot pot. This is known as a 'reflex arc'. This process happens so fast that the response occurs before the message reaches the brain or the message may not be sent to the brain at all.

187. Sense Organs

Sense organs connect a human body to the external environment by the means of five senses: vision, smell, taste, hearing and touch. These sense organs work in coordination with the nervous system. Hence, the central nervous system is responsible for sensing the external environments and responding accordingly. Each sense organ has specific receptors in the human brain that react to specific stimuli. For example: Receptors of vision, hearing, touch, smell and taste. These sensory receptors are connected with specific nerve endings that collect the stimuli from those sense organs.

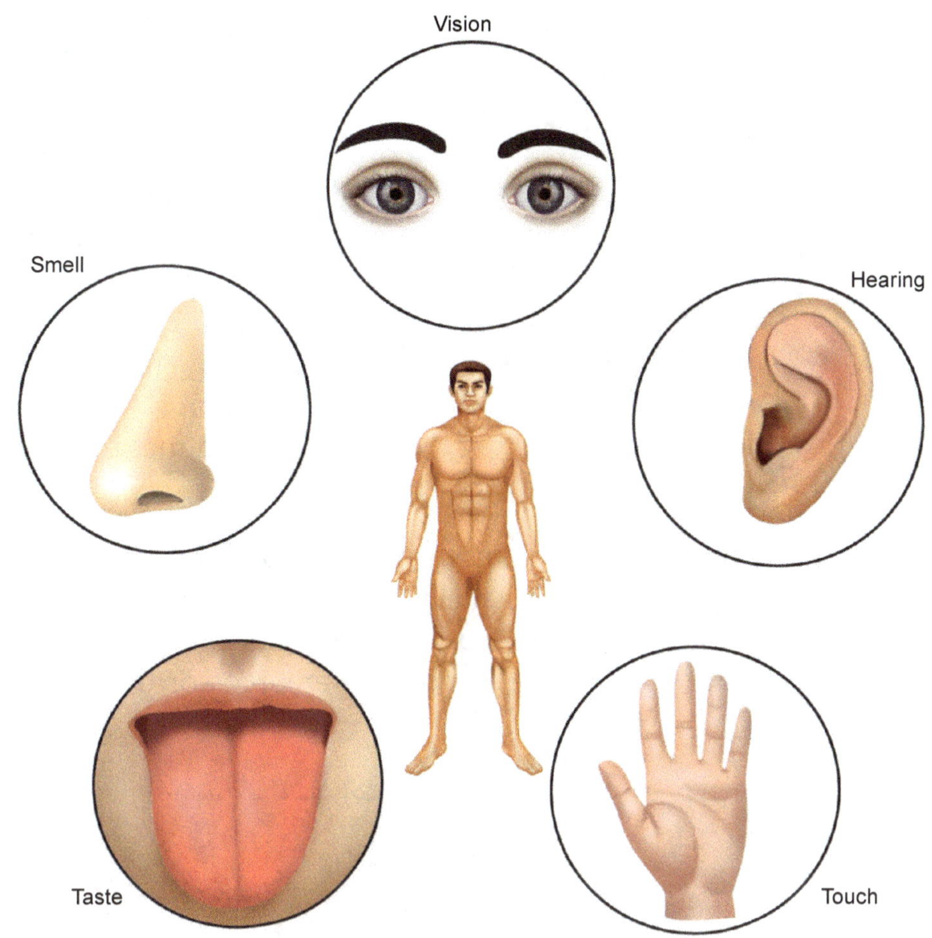

188. Eye

The eye is a delicate organ; it is the sense organ for vision. Eyes are connected with the optic nerves. The eye sockets of the skull in which the eyes are present are lined by soft tissues. Eyelids, eyelashes, eyebrows and tears protect the eye from dust and dirt. The special cells known as photo receptors provide visual information to the eyes with the help of cones and rods, located in the back of the eye. The main parts of the eye are: cornea, iris, pupil, lens and retina.

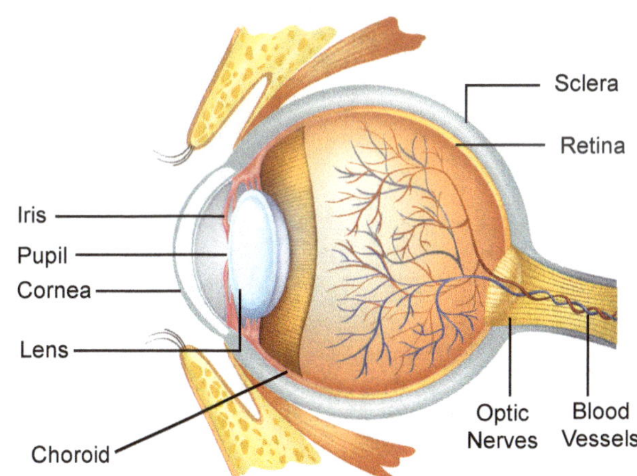

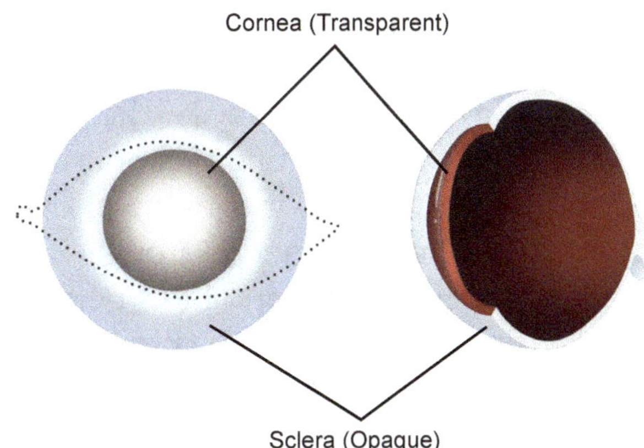

189. Sclera and Cornea

Sclera (white portion of the eye) is the outer sheath of the eyeball. Sclera protects the eye from damage as it is the toughest pigmented fibrous coat of the eye. Sclera consists of an inner circular muscle and an outer radial muscle. Sclera controls the amount of light entering the eye. The cornea is the transparent outermost layer of the eye. It is also referred as a transparent 'window'. It is the main part through which light enters the eye.

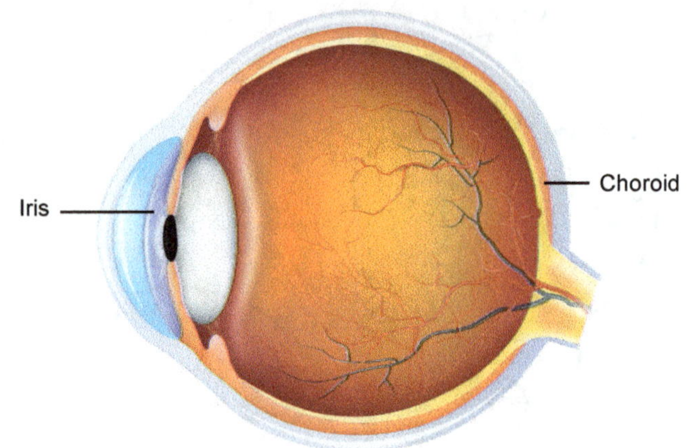

190. Choroid and Iris

Choroid is the middle layer located just after the sclera. Choroid is supplied with blood vessels and it forms the iris. There is a central opening in the choroid layer, the pupil. The main function of the choroid is to supply nutrients and oxygen to the sclera and the retina. The iris is a thin, circular membrane in the eye. It has a pigmented layer behind it, which imparts a specific colour to the eye. The iris muscles help relax and contract the pupil.

191. Pupil

Both the eyes and the camera have a black dot in the centre. This black dot helps capture an image. In case of the eye, it is called the pupil which is an opening on the iris. It lets the light fall on the retina and acts as a regulator, i.e. it regulates the amount of light falling on the retina. The pupil shrinks when the light is very bright and enlarges or opens wide when the light is dim.

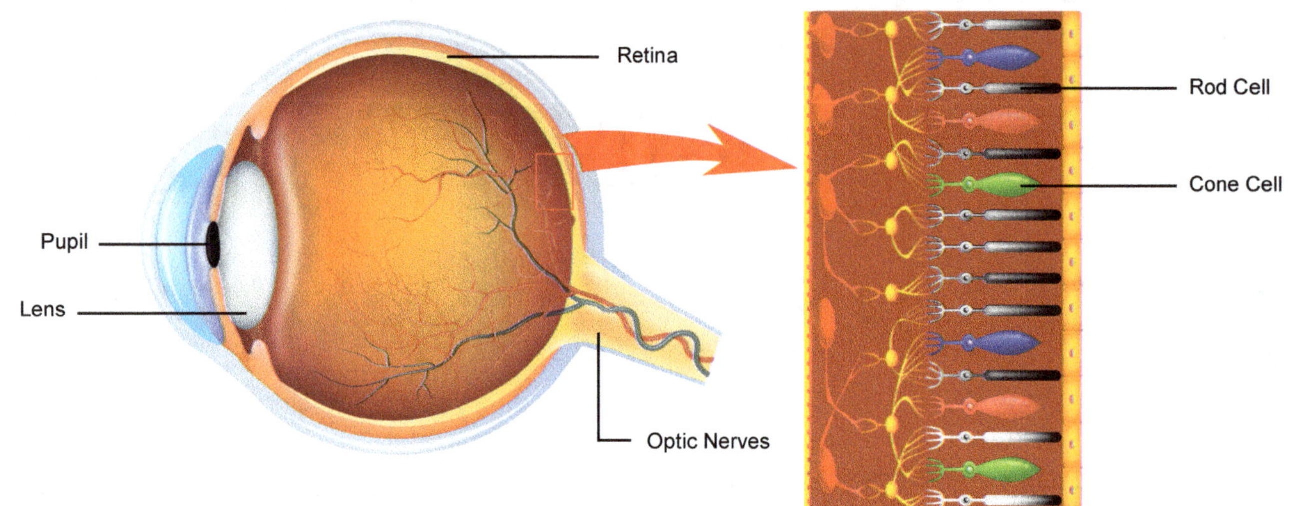

192. Retina

The retina is the innermost layer of the eyeball. It is composed of several layers of nerve fibres. In the retina, light is converted into electrical impulses with the help of the photo receptors (rod and cones) that are connected with the nerves of the brain. Rod cells are responsible for black-and-white vision in faint light and cones are responsible for colour vision.

193. Lens

The lens is a transparent biconvex structure inside the eye. It is located behind the iris. There is no blood supply in the lens. These cells receive nutrients from the surrounding fluids. The lens is flexible in nature due to the ciliary muscles that surround it. The flexibility of the lens enables it to see distant as well as closer objects. The main function of the lens is to help to focus the light on the retina.

194. Optic Nerves

Optic nerves (cranial nerves II) as the name suggests, are the connection between the eye and the brain. They are located at the back of the eye. The optic nerve is made of ganglionic cells or nerve cells. It consists of over one million nerve fibres. The principal function of this nerve is to transfer visual information from the retina to the vision centres of the brain via electrical impulses.

Image formation by an eye is based on the passage of light in the eye. It is an instant process.

1. Firstly, the light enters the eye and passes through the transparent cornea to the pupil in the centre of the iris.

2. Then, the adjustable lens and the fixed cornea focus the light rays on the retina to form a clear image.

3. The entire image formation process depends on the nerve signals. The optical nerves present in the eye convey the image as an electrical impulse towards the brain. The optic centres of the brain process the image formation and a clear image is formed on the retina.

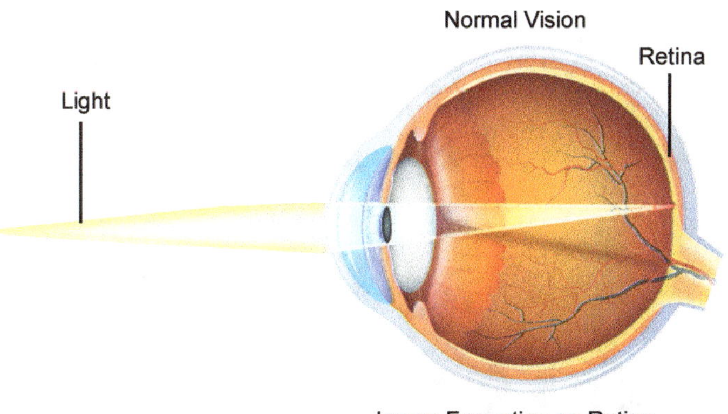

Image Formation on Retina

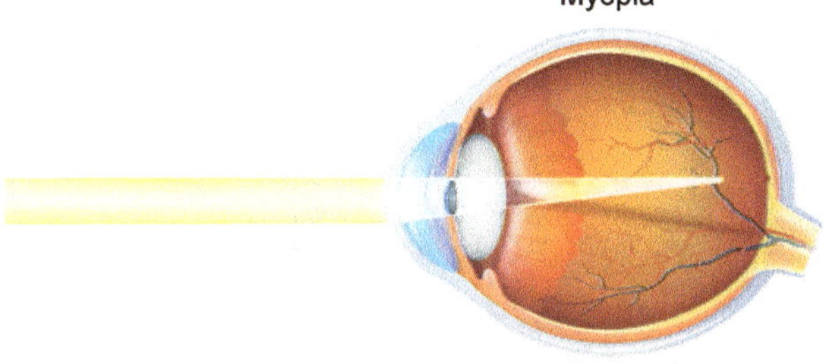

Image Formation in front of Retina

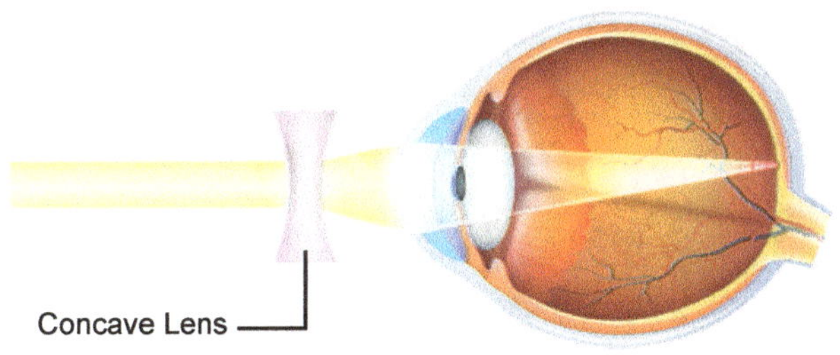

Myopia Corrected

Myopia

Myopia is a common visual deformity. It is also known as nearsightedness or short sightedness. In myopia, the eye focuses better on the objects that are nearer than the objects which are at a farther distance. In this visual disorder, a person has enlarged eyeballs or excessively curved cornea. This physiological defect alters the image formation and focus of light rays through the lens on the retina. In general, this defect occurs in school-going children when the eyeball is developing. It progresses up to 20 years of age.

Hypermetropia

Hypermetropia is another visual disorder. It is also known as long-sightedness or far-sightedness. In this condition, the eye focuses better on distant objects than nearby objects, hence nearby objects appear blurred (this is just opposite to myopia). Physiologically, a person presenting this disorder has smaller eyeballs than the normal size or cornea with smaller curvature. Due to this defect, the lens focuses the image behind the retina.

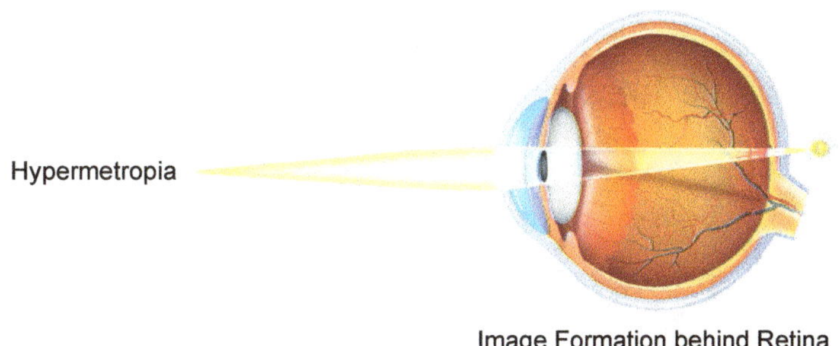

Image Formation behind Retina

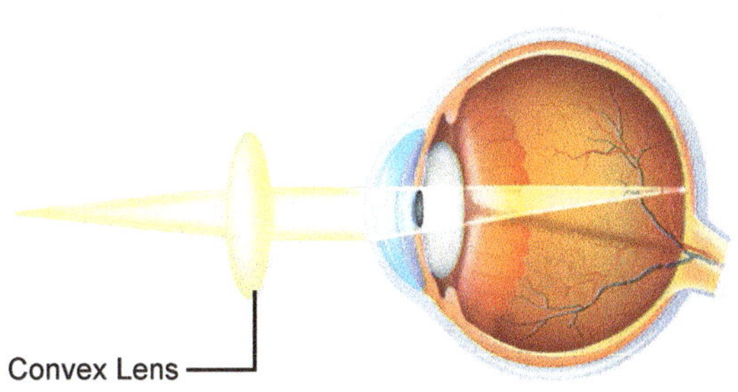

Hypermetropia Corrected

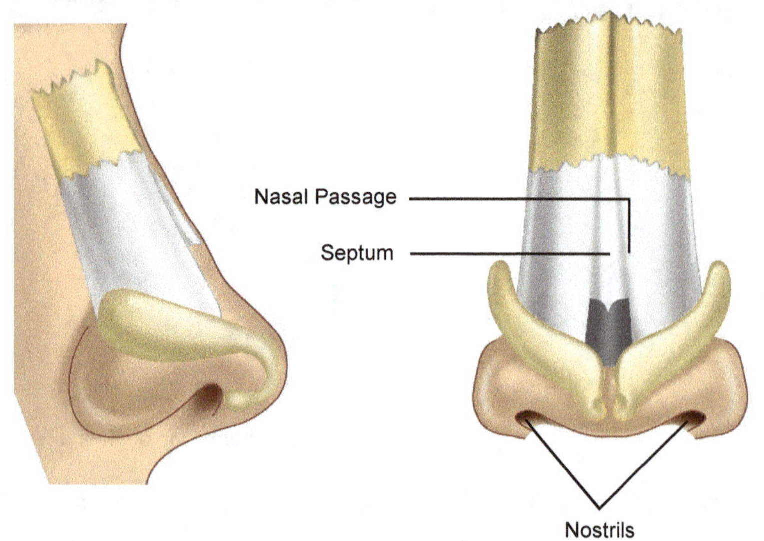

195. Nose

The nose is the sense organ for smell. It is connected with the olfactory nerves of the brain. The nose helps a person to smell and carry out one of the most important functions called the respiration. It works in coordination with the sense of taste. The main parts of the nose are: the two nostrils, a nasal passage and the nasal cavity. The two nostrils are divided by a wall called the septum.

196. Nasal Cavity

The nose has an internal air-filled chamber called the nasal cavity. Septum divides the nasal cavity into two sections. The septum walls consist of two skull bones: the ethmoid above and the nasal concha (below). Nasal cavity is connected with the throat. On the upper wall or the roof of the nasal cavity, the olfactory bulb and the olfactory nerves are located. The palate in the mouth divides the nasal cavity and the mouth.

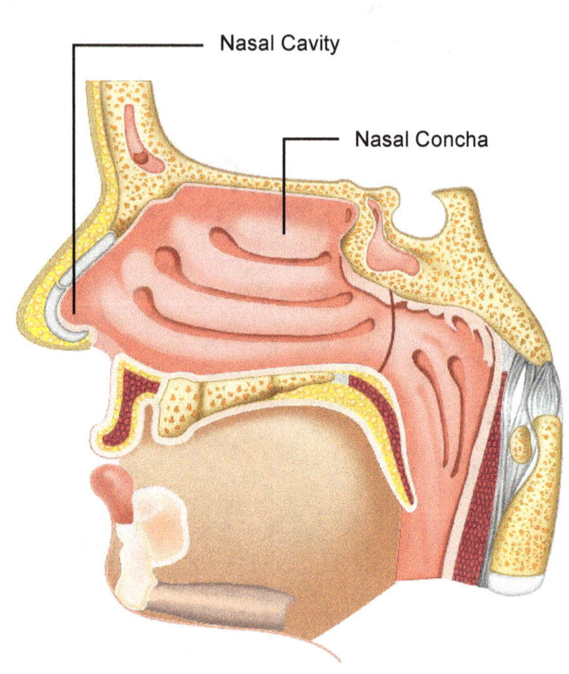

197. Olfactory Portion

The olfactory portion of the nose is exclusively involved in the sensation of smell. The olfactory portion of the nose consists of: the olfactory epithelium, olfactory nerves and olfactory bulb. The olfactory epithelium is a soft patch on the roof of the nasal cavity. This epithelium has several olfactory hair cells connected to the olfactory bulb. The olfactory bulb extends towards the olfactory nerves. The olfactory nerves convey signal to the olfactory centres of the brain where the smell/odour is identified.

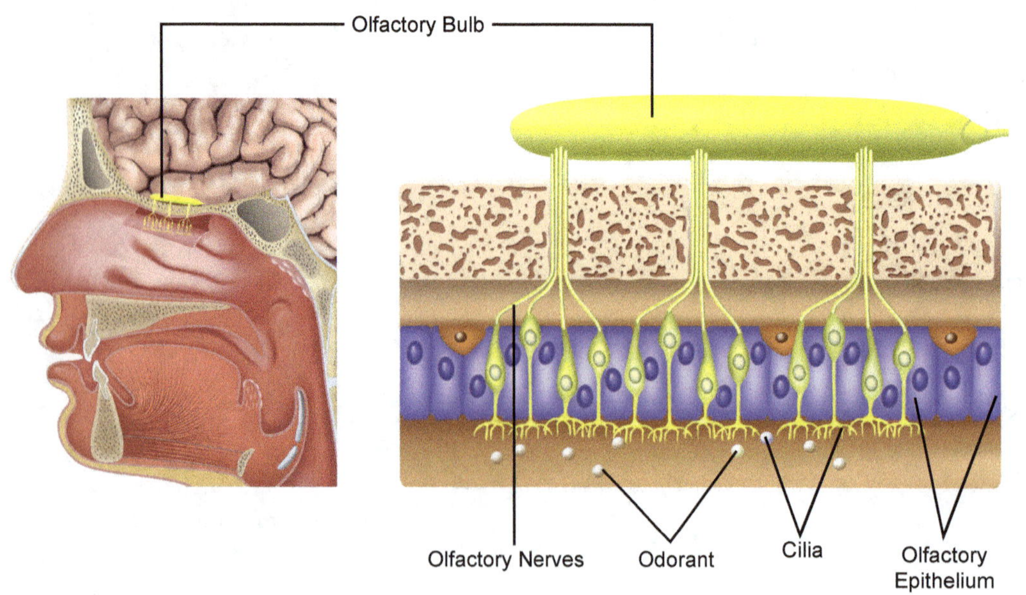

198. Ear

The human ear is a hearing organ designed to collect sound vibrations, and then pass those vibrations to the brain through auditory nerves. The main part of the ear is located inside the skull. The ear has a complex structure; it has several small bones intricately arranged inside it. It has the smallest bone of the body, the stapes. The sound waves from the outer ear travel to the middle ear. Through the bones and ear-drum, it travels to the innermost part, the bony labyrinth.

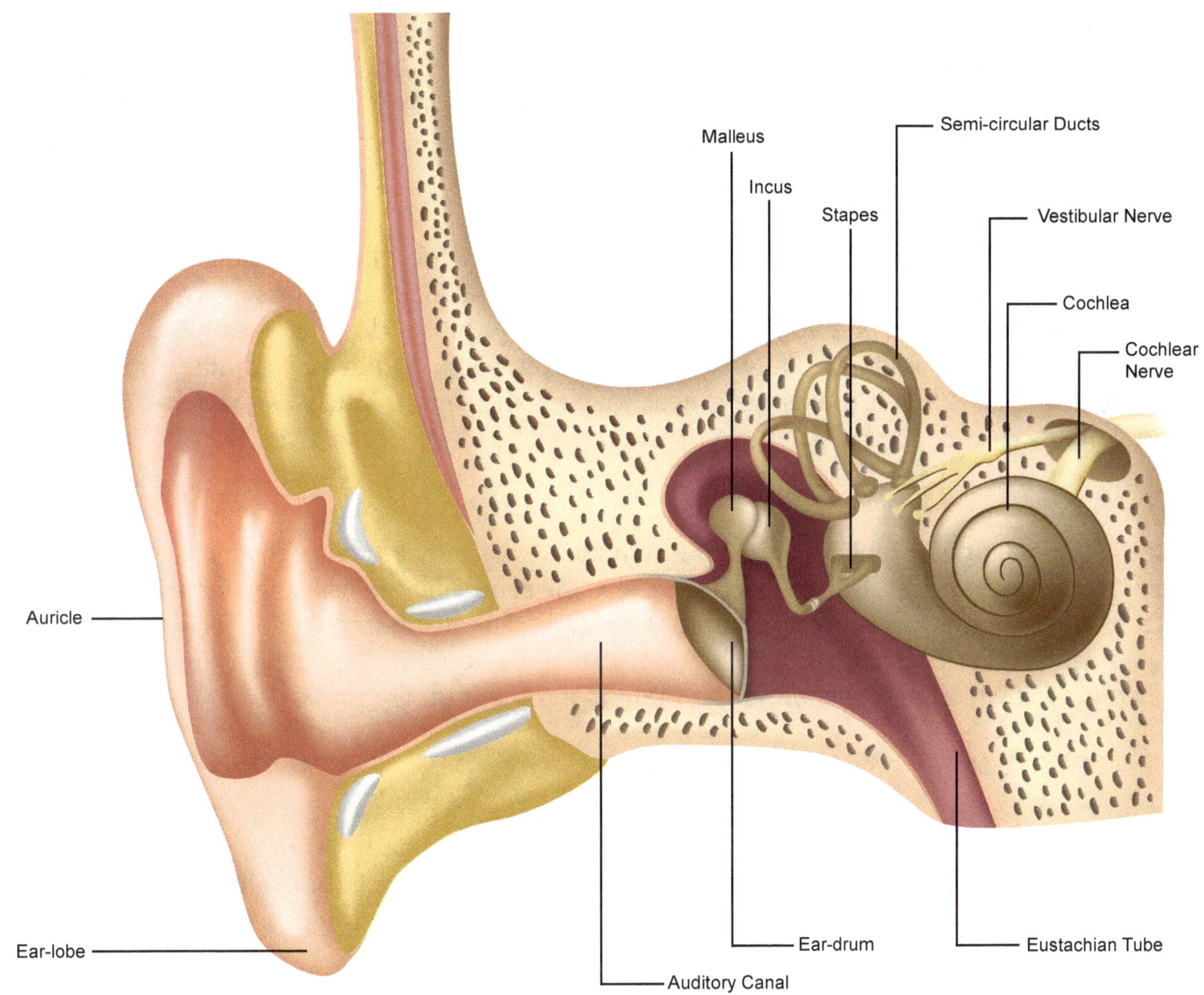

199. External Ear

The external ear, also called the auricle or pinna, is divided into the following parts: the pinna and external auditory meatus. It is a funnel that collects the sound vibrations. The collected sound vibrations travel through a large membrane present at the end of the external ear. The irregularly shaped auricle is made up of cartilage and fibrous tissues. The narrow entrance of the ear is called the concha. The ear canal has wax and hair to trap dirt that could harm the internal ear.

200. Ear-drum

The ear-drum is a thin membrane present at the interface of the outer ear and the middle ear. This membrane acts as a drum, which is beaten by sound waves. It is connected with a set of three small bones. It is an important as well as a crucial part of the ear which helps a human being to hear. When the ear-drum receives a sound, it vibrates to and fro. These vibrations are received by the auditory nerves and are eventually transferred to the brain as signals.

201. Middle Ear

The middle ear is the connection between the external ear and the inner ear. The ear-drum is placed at the entrance of the middle ear. The middle ear has ear bones (ossicles) which act as small levers that work together to relay the sound vibration. These bones are: malleus, incus and stapes. At the end of the bones is the tympanic cavity and eustachian tube. This tube regulates air pressure in the ear.

202. Eustachian Tube

Eustachian tube, also called the auditory tube, is a narrow tube that connects middle ear to the throat. It is an important part of the human ear. This tube balances the pressure of the air on both sides of the ear-drum. This equilibrium can be disturbed by the sudden changes in air pressure that can be experienced while diving underwater or while travelling in aircraft. Another important task performed by this tube is that it drains the mucus towards the throat. Mucus is produced by the lining of the middle ear.

203. Cochlea

Cochlea is the main part of the inner ear. It resembles a snail's shell. The cochlea is filled with a liquid and lined with many nerve cells. It is designed to receive the sound vibrations. When the eardrum vibrates, the vibrations are, in turn, passed along the three small bones of the middle ear. The last bone of the middle ear is set into the cochlea, so the vibrations cause the liquid in the cochlea to move and sweep over the nerve cells, which send signals to the brain along the auditory nerve.

204. Inner Ear

The innermost part of the ear is the inner ear. The main parts of the inner ear are the oval window and the bony labyrinth. The bony labyrinth is further divided into three parts: the vestibule, the cochlea and the semi-circular canals. The inner ear is filled with a liquid. The cochlea is the most important part as it converts sound vibrations into nerve signals. The internal ear is innervated with auditory nerves.

Head Balancing Fluid in the Ear

The innermost semi-circular canals of the ear have fluid in it. This fluid is very important for balancing the position and movement of the head. This fluid moves when our head moves or rotates. The movement of the fluid sends signals to the brain about the direction and speed of the rotation of the head. When we spin our head continuously for a few minutes and suddenly stop, we feel dizzy. This is because when the head is spun fast, the fluid in the canals also starts moving and sustains the movement even after the head has stopped its movement. The movement of the fluid sends signal to the brain about the spinning of the head. This, in turn, confuses the brain, because the head has stopped rotating but the ear fluid is sending signals regarding the rotations. As a result, we start feeling dizzy.

205. Auditory Nerves

The auditory nerves transmit the sound wave from the ear-drum to the auditory centre in the brain. These auditory nerves (VIII cranial nerve) are made by the association of vestibular nerve and the cochlear nerve.

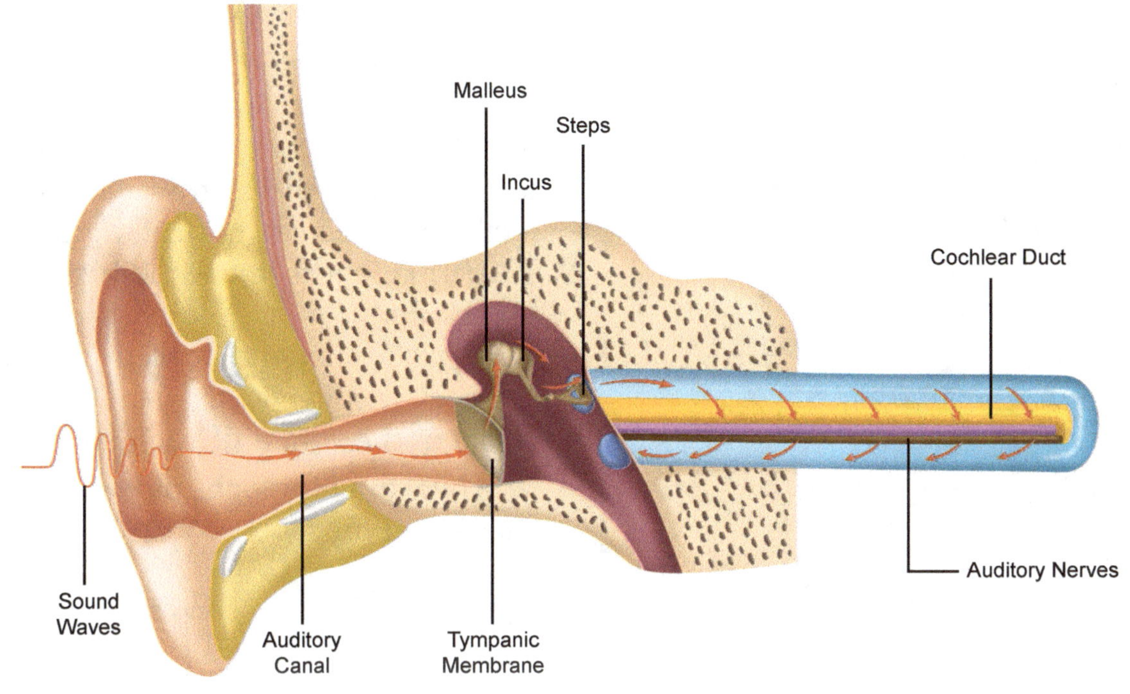

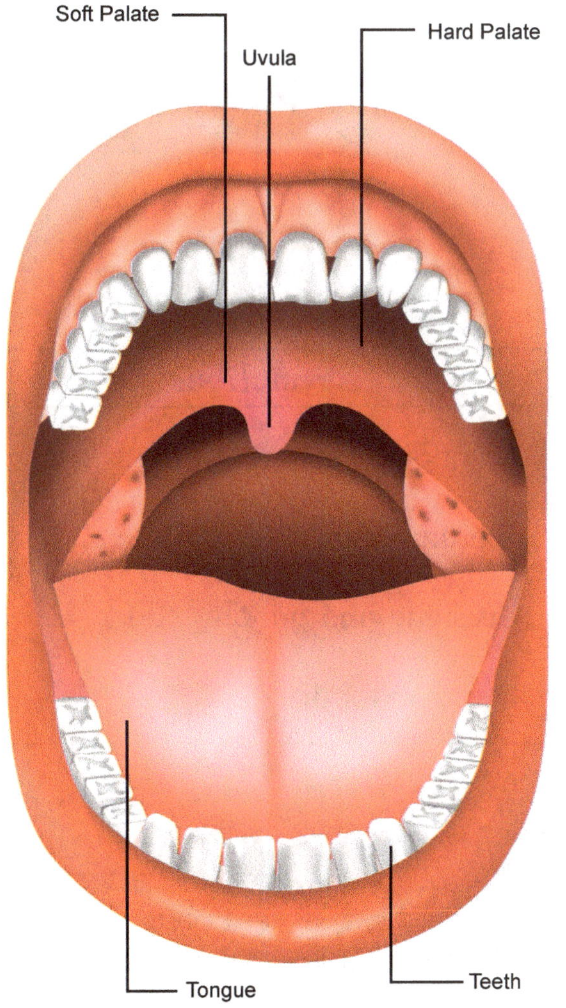

206. Mouth

The mouth is a hollow oral cavity located below the nose and works in close coordination with the nose. It serves several purposes, such as ingestion of food, detection of taste and digestion. The mouth cavity has many organs inside it: it starts with lips and inside it, it contains other organs, like the teeth, tongue (taste organ) and the salivary glands, hard and soft palates and the throat. The tongue is the sense organ for taste as it has taste buds on it.

207. Soft and Hard Palate

Palate is the upper portion of the mouth near the back of the throat. It is divided into two parts: soft palate and hard palate. Soft palate is made of muscles and connective tissues. A small organ called the uvula is present at the back side of the soft palate. The soft palate muscles help swallow the food, by pushing it down towards the throat. Hard palate is the bony part of the mouth roof that separates the nose from the mouth.

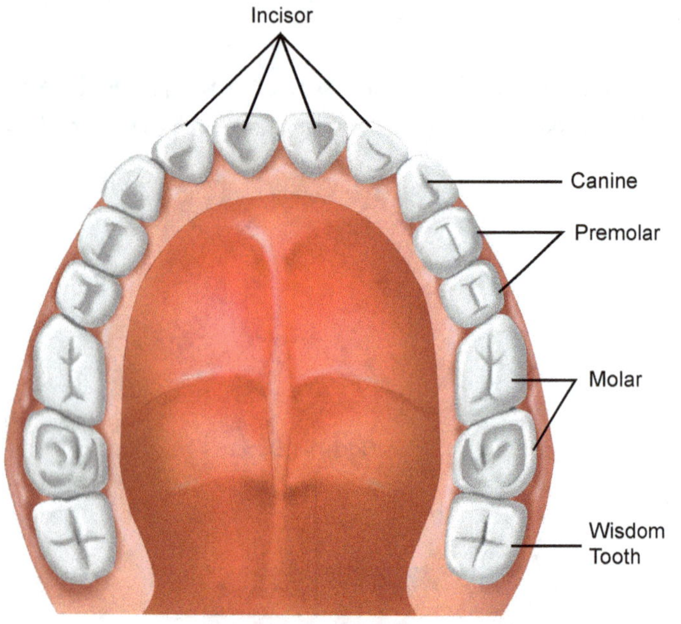

208. Teeth

Teeth are the hard, bony structures that are fixed in deep sockets in the jawbone. These sockets are attached to the jawbone with the help of strong periodontal fibres and cementum.

A human being possesses two sets of teeth during the entire lifetime, the temporary set and the permanent set. An infant has 20 temporary teeth or milk teeth which are replaced by permanent teeth eventually as the child grows. An adult has 32 permanent teeth. A tooth possesses a crown, a neck and a root. A tooth is made up of a very hard white material called the enamel which encloses a softer layer, dentine. There is a pulp cavity in the centre of each tooth.

There are four types of teeth according to their shape and function.

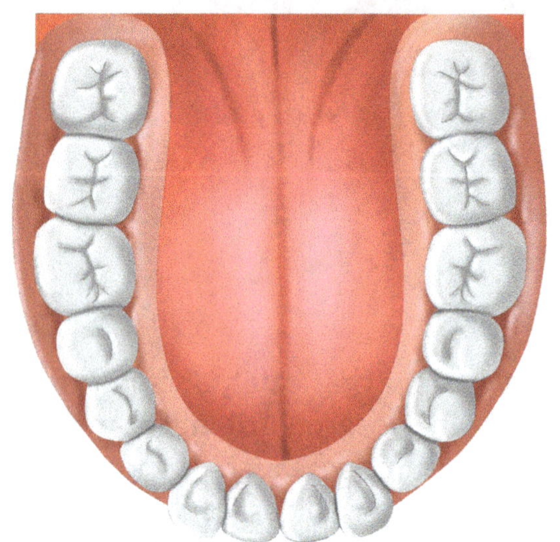

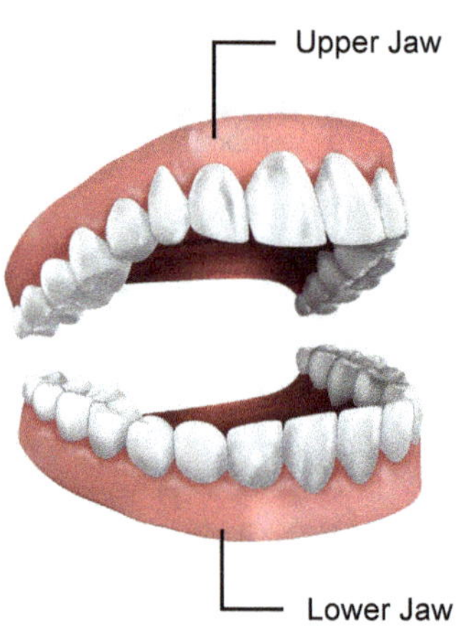

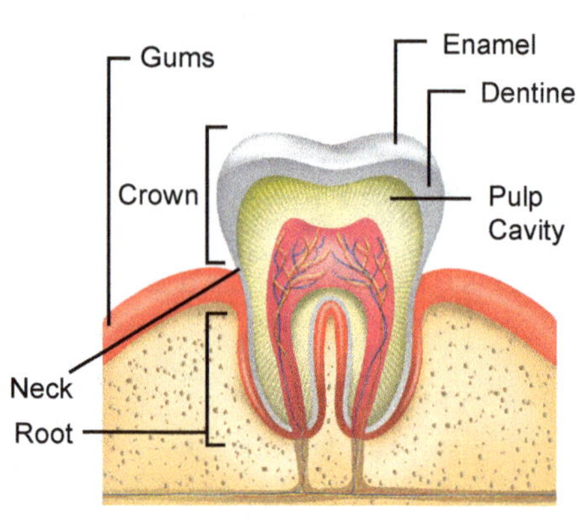

Types of teeth	Shapes	Functions
A. Incisor (8)	Chisel-shaped with sharp flat ends	Cutting and chopping food
B. Canine (4)	Pointed sharp teeth	Tearing flesh
C. Premolar (8)	Big-sized, flat and ridge-topped	Crushing and grinding food
D. Molar (12)	Toughest teeth, ridge-topped	Grinding food

Wisdom Tooth

After the age of twenty, four more molar grow at the back side of the jaw, one on each corner. These teeth are not of much importance. The eruption of a wisdom tooth is very painful as by the time it erupts the jaw tissues of grown-up adults become hard. Some people get their wisdom teeth pulled out by a dentist.

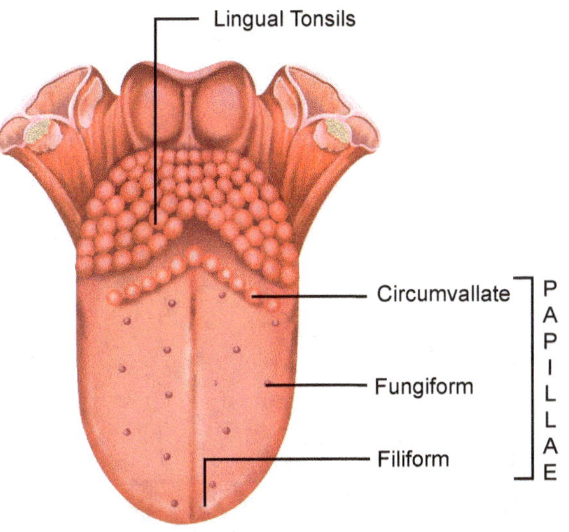

209. Tongue

The tongue is the sense organ for taste. It is made up of several muscle elements and is a flexible part. It has two types of muscles, one of the muscles that performs delicate movements and the other that performs larger movements (mastication and swallowing). The tongue is attached to the throat and is placed on the hyoid bone. It contains the following parts: the papillae, taste buds and lingual tonsils. The papillae are present on the upper surface and the sense of taste is associated with them.

210. Papillae

Papillae are very small finger-like projections located on the surface of the tongue. There are three kinds of papillae on the tongue surface: circumvallate, fungiform and filiform. Circumvallate (8-12 in number) are the largest papillae located at the back side of the tongue; they are round in shape. Fungiform are small mushroom-like projections at the tip and the sides of the tongue and filiform are the most abundant papillae covering the entire surface of the tongue. All papillae contain taste buds, except the filiform.

211. Taste Buds

Taste buds are the taste receptors present on the tongue; they are the tiny sensory structures. They are located around the base of the papillae. There are numerous taste buds on the circumvallate and the fungiform papillae. There are four types of taste buds according to the tastes–bitter sensing buds are located at the back, sweet at the front tip, sour at the back and salty at the sides of the tongue. Taste buds are connected to a main nerve by a bundle of nerve fibres.

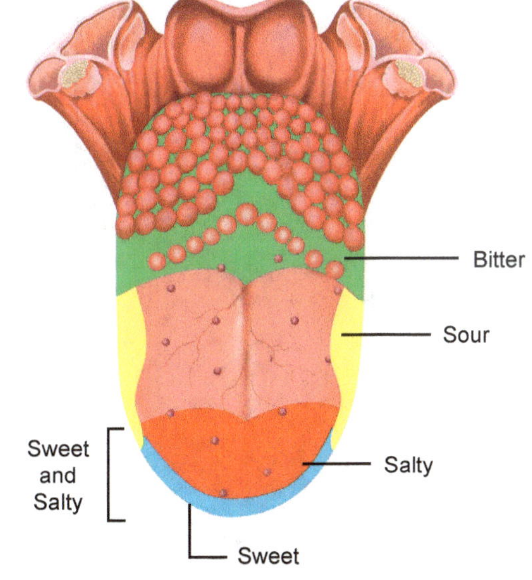

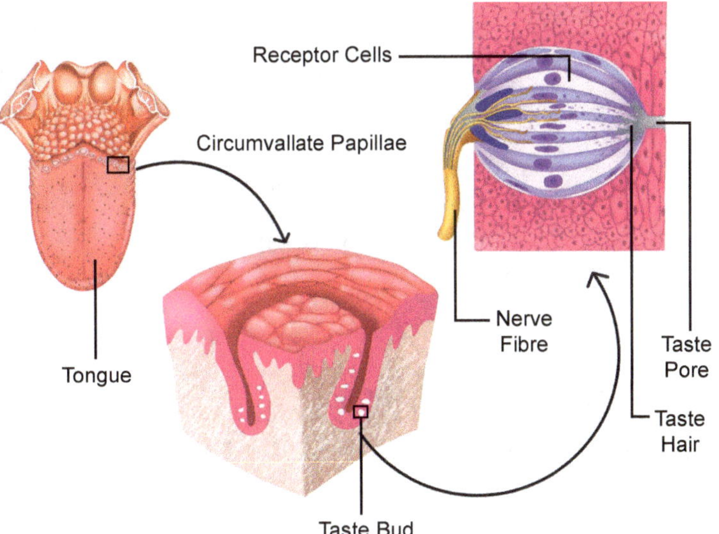

212. Taste Pores and Nerves

The taste pores are envelope-shaped structures that house taste buds, supporting cells and nerve endings of taste nerves. The taste sensations are transmitted to the taste nerves through the taste pores. The tongue is connected with the V, VII and IX cranial nerves that are responsible for the overall taste sensation perception. The taste centre is located in the gustatory cortex of the brain.

213. Skin

Skin is the outer covering of the body; it is one of the largest organs of the human body. It is the sense organ of touch, but plays certain crucial roles such as: regulation of body temperature and waste excretion. Skin along with hair and nails form the integumentary system. They provide external protection to the body. Skin is composed of three layers: the epidermis, dermis and hypodermis (subcutaneous layer). Skin colour depends on a pigment named melanin present in the epidermal layer.

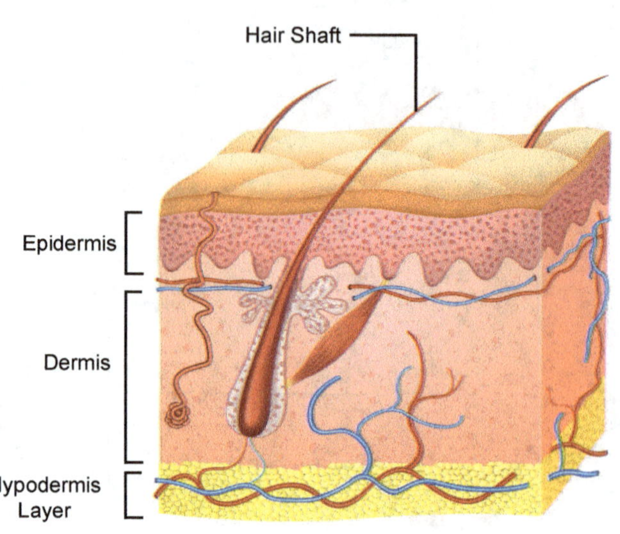

214. Epidermis

The epidermis is the outermost layer of the skin. It is called the protective layer of the skin, as it protects the body from the harmful ultraviolet rays. This layer is composed of thin and flat cells and dead cells. The epidermis contains two layers: the stratum corneum and basal layer. The stratum corneum is relatively waterproof and safeguards skin from microbial invasion. Basal layer is located above the dermis and has the colour pigments melanin in it.

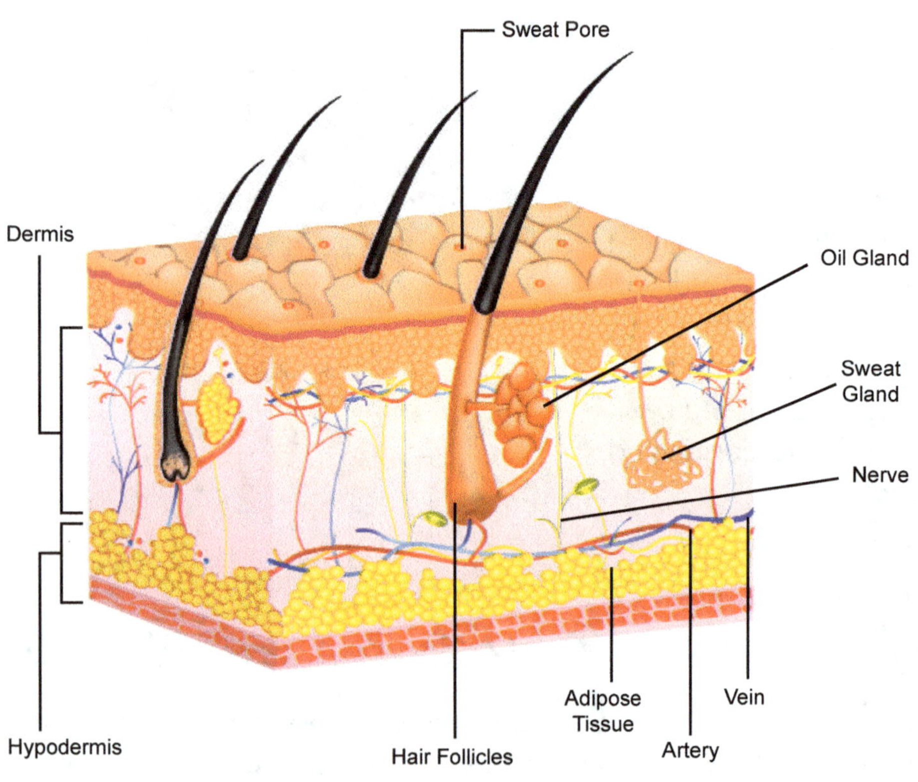

215. Dermis

Dermis is the thicker middle layer of the skin. It is composed of fibrous connective tissues. This layer has several microstructures, such as: blood vessels, hair follicles and glands that produce sweat, hair follicles and nail. These microstructures are supplied by arteries and veins. This layer also acts as a base for several sensory nerves and receptors. The sensory receptors perceive pain, touch and temperature. The sweat glands control body temperature.

216. Hypodermis Layer

The hypodermis layer is the innermost layer of the skin. This layer is also referred as the subcutaneous layer. It is mainly composed of adipose tissues. Adipose tissues are the loose connective tissues and fatty material. In some places, these tissues are thicker. These thicker tissues form fatty pads. The main function of this layer is to provide protection to the inner organs, to store energy as body fat and to insulate the body.

217. Glands

The skin layers have various glands, the sweat gland and fat/sebaceous glands, found throughout the body, except a few areas like, the palms of the hands and soles of the feet. The sweat glands secrete mostly a concentrated salty sweat into the gland tube that lowers the body temperature, especially in summer season. The fat or the sebaceous glands that are mainly found on the face and the scalp secrete fat called the sebum. The sebum lubricates the skin.

218. Pores

The skin layers have various pores. Sweat glands open onto the surface as pores, also called the sweat pores. The sweat pores are the minute ducts through which sweat comes out of the skin layer. Pores are important for maintaining a healthy skin. If the pores are blocked due to dirt and oil, it creates a pile-up of oil and dead skin cells in the follicle.

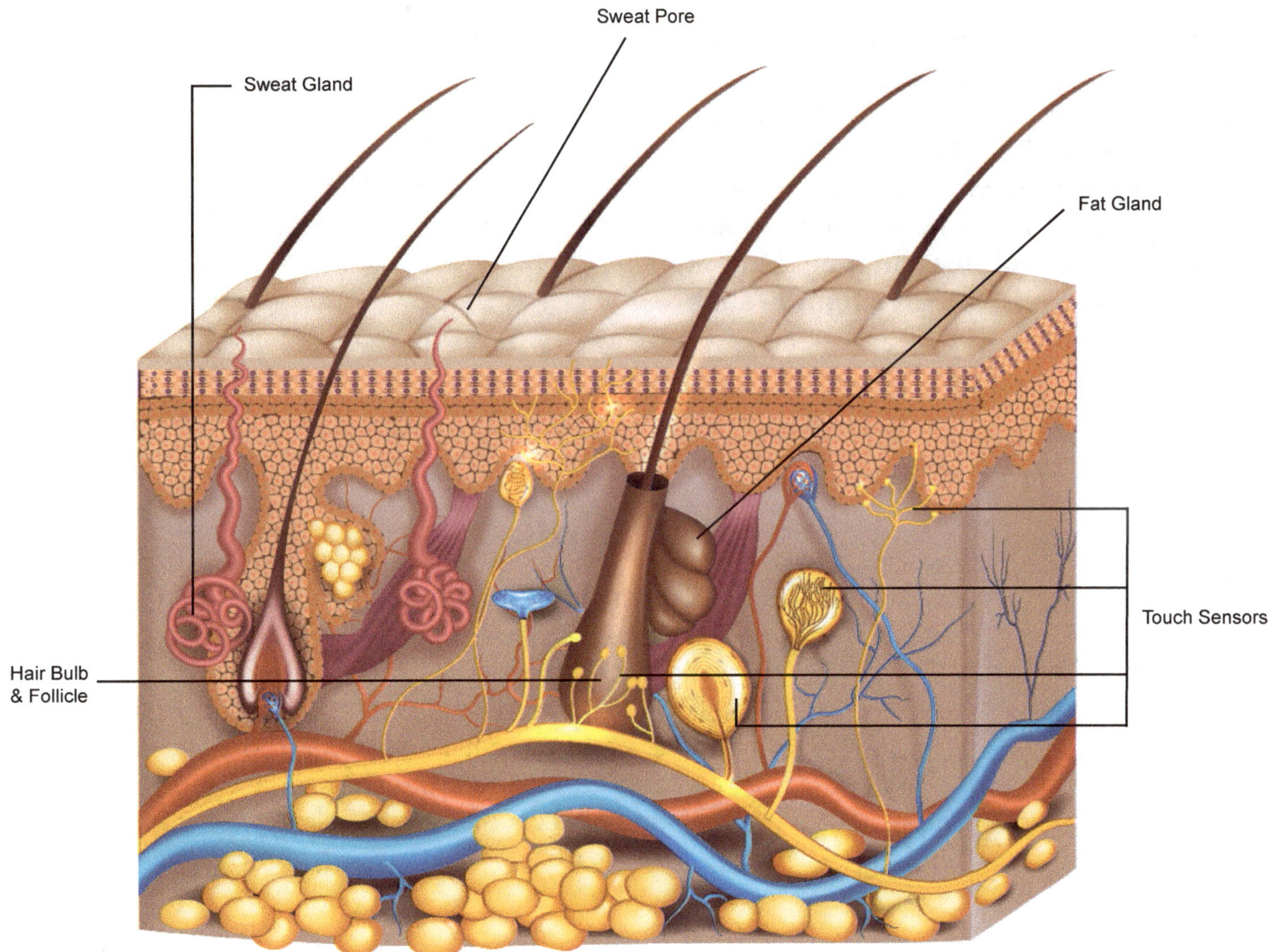

219. Touch Sensors

Skin is the sense organ of touch. The sense of touch is perceived by a network of touch sensors. The sensors are basically specialised nerve fibre endings. These sensors are distributed at specific depths in the dermis layer. The location of the sensor defines the type of sensation they would perceive. A few of them detect only some specific stimuli including very light touch and reduction in temperature.

220. Hair

Hair is a type of modified epidermal layer. The hair follicles are embedded deep in the dermis layer of the skin, from where hair growth takes place. Hair falling and growth is a continuous process. Hair is composed of dead cells which contain the protein keratin. The parts of the hair are: tip, shaft, root and follicle. Hair provides protection to the head and the entire body. They keep the head warm and the hair in the eyelash protects the eye from dust.

Human hair is an unusual creation. It has a long lifespan that is around 3 to 7 years. Human hair possesses one more interesting quality, i.e. it is virtually indestructible. It decays at a very slow rate. It cannot be destroyed by cold, change of climate, water or other natural resources, though it is susceptible to heat and fire. It has also been observed that human hair is resistant to several corrosive liquids such as toilet cleaners.

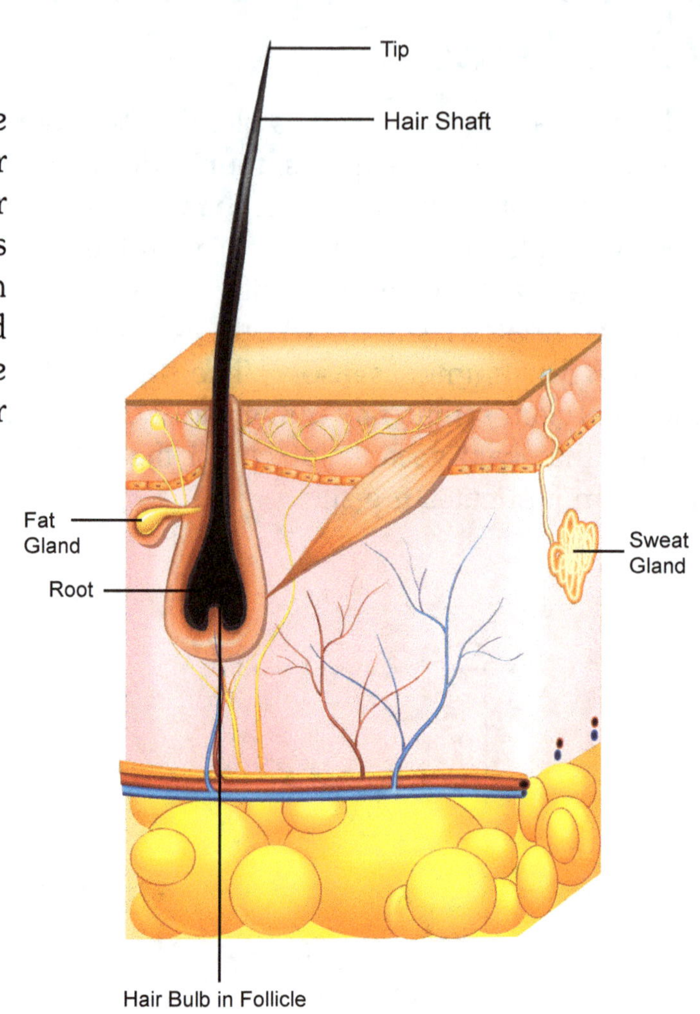

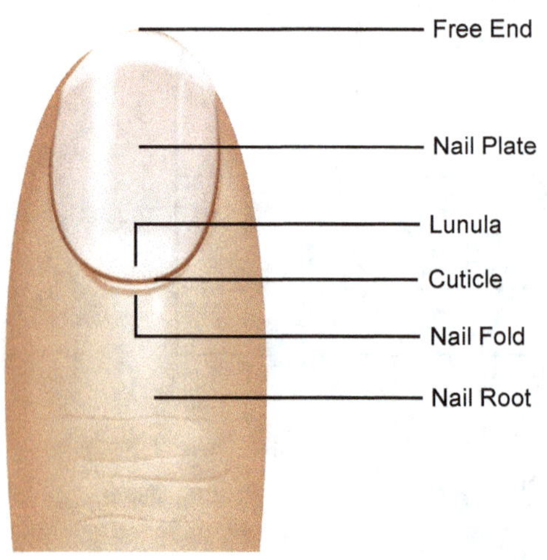

221. Nail

Nail is basically a modified form of skin. Nails are the hard coverings that protect the fingers and the toes. They are composed of keratin and are made by the epidermal cells. The parts of a nail are: free end, main nail plate, lunula, nail fold, cuticle and nail root. The nail is a dead part and cannot feel pain. The pain is felt through the surrounding skin of the nail. Nail helps grip, scratch and pick things up.

Nail is a tough protective shield for fingers and toes. It is a dead part of the human body, but it has its own significance. Although the entire human nail is not dead yet some part of the nail is alive. The part of the nail that is alive is its innermost part which is covered under the skin (epidermis). This live part is the part that grows continuously. Human nails keep on growing throughout the lifespan. The rate of the growth of a human nail depends on the length of the outermost finger bones (phalanges). This is the reason why the nail of the index figure in a human grows faster than the little finger.